European Communities

INTERNATIONAL ORGANIZATIONS SERIES

General Editors:
Robert G. Neville (Executive Editor)
John J. Horton

Robert A. Myers   John Paxton
Ian Wallace   Hans H. Wellisch

John J. Horton is Deputy Librarian of the University of Bradford and currently Chairman of its Academic Board of Studies in Social Sciences. He has maintained a longstanding interest in the discipline of area studies and its associated bibliographical problems, with special reference to European Studies. In particular he has published in the field of Icelandic and of Yugoslav studies, including the two relevant volumes in the World Bibliographical Series.

Robert A. Myers is Associate Professor of Anthropology in the Division of Social Sciences and Director of Study Abroad Programs at Alfred University, Alfred, New York. He has studied post-colonial island nations of the Caribbean and has spent two years in Nigeria on a Fulbright Lectureship. His interests include international public health, historical anthropology and developing societies. In addition to *Amerindians of the Lesser Antilles: a bibliography* (1981), *A Resource Guide to Dominica, 1493–1986* (1987) and numerous articles, he has compiled the World Bibliographical Series volumes on *Dominica* (1987), *Nigeria* (1989) and *Ghana* (1991).

John Paxton was the editor of *The Statesman's Year-Book* from 1969 to 1990. His published works include *The Developing Common Market, The Dictionary of the European Communities* (which was commended by the McColvin Medal Committee of the British Library Association), *The Penguin Dictionary of Abbreviations, The Penguin Dictionary of Proper Names* (with G. Paton), *Companion to Russian History, Companion to the French Revolution*, and *The Statesman's Year-Book Gazetteer*. He was also chief consultant editor of the *New Illustrated Everyman's Encyclopaedia*.

Ian Wallace is Professor of German at the University of Bath. A graduate of Oxford in French and German, he also studied in Tübingen, Heidelberg and Lausanne before taking teaching posts at universities in the USA, Scotland and England. He specializes in contemporary German affairs, especially literature and culture, on which he has published numerous articles and books. In 1979 he founded the journal *GDR Monitor*, which he continues to edit under its new title *German Monitor*.

Hans H. Wellisch is Professor emeritus at the College of Library and Information Services, University of Maryland. He was President of the American Society of Indexers and was a member of the International Federation for Documentation. He is the author of numerous articles and several books on indexing and abstracting, and has published *The Conversion of Scripts* and *Indexing and Abstracting: an International Bibliography*. He also contributes frequently to *Journal of the American Society for Information Science, The Indexer* and other professional journals.

VOLUME 1

European Communities

John Paxton
Compiler

Transaction Publishers
NEW BRUNSWICK (U.S.A.) AND LONDON (U.K.)

© Copyright 1992 by Clio Press Ltd.

Library of Congress Cataloging-in-Publication Data

Paxton, John.
European communities / John Paxton.
p.cm.—(International organizations : v. 1)
Includes index.
ISBN 1–56000–052–X
1. European Economic Community—Bibliography.2. European
Economic Community countries—Economic policy—Bibliography.
3. European Economic Community countries—Politics and government—
Bibliography.I. Title.II. Series.
Z7165.E8P341992
[HC241.2]
016.34124′22—dc20   91–41792
CIP

Library of Congress Catalog Number: 91–41792
ISBN: 1–56000–052–X
Printed in the United States of America

Transaction Publishers
Rutgers University
New Brunswick
NJ 08903

INTERNATIONAL ORGANIZATIONS SERIES

Each volume in the International Organizations Series is either devoted to one specific organization, or to a number of different organizations operating in a particular region, or engaged in a specific field of activity. The scope of the series is wide-ranging and includes intergovernmental organizations, international non-governmental organizations, and national bodies dealing with international issues. The series is aimed mainly at the English-speaker and each volume provides a selective, annotated, critical bibliography of the organization, or organizations, concerned. The bibliographies cover books, articles, pamphlets, directories, databases and theses and, wherever possible, attention is focused on material *about* the organizations rather than on the organizations' own publications. Notwithstanding this, the most important official publications, and guides to those publications, will be included. The views expressed in individual volumes, however, are not necessarily those of the publishers.

VOLUMES IN THE SERIES

1 *European Communities*,
John Paxton
2 *Arab Regional Organizations*,
Frank A. Clements

3 *Comecon: The Rise and Fall of an International Socialist Organization*, Jenny Brine
4 *International Monetary Fund*,
Anne C. M. Salda

TITLES IN PREPARATION

Organization of African Unity,
Gordon Harris
French Secret Services, Martyn Cornick
and Peter Morris
Commonwealth, Patricia Larby and
Harry Hannam

North Atlantic Treaty Organization,
Phil Williams
Organization of American States,
David Sheinin
Israeli Secret Services,
Frank A. Clements
World Bank, Anne C. M. Salda

Cherrill, George, Joseph, Samuel and Thomas
the new
Europeans

Contents

Contents

Introduction

The Treaty of Rome came into force on 1 January 1958 and is one of the most remarkable documents in the social and economic history of the Western world. It is explicit in providing for a complete economic union so that goods, people and capital will be able to pass over national boundaries of member countries as freely as they can move inside any one country today.

For several decades most of the words written about the European Economic Community were concerned with international and European trade, and indeed the expression 'Common Market' was unfortunate because the general public could well believe that the EEC was just a customs union. It is far more than that – as we shall see as the debate intensifies on monetary and political union. Walter Hallstein, the first President of the Commission said 'Make no mistake about it, we are not in business, we are in politics.'

Progress towards the Treaty of Rome's objectives since 1958 has, at times, been slow and apathy has dominated. At other times rows over agriculture and budgets kept the writers busy. The surprising lurch forward in the evolution of the Treaty's aims came in December 1985 with the signing of the Single European Act and from then on journalists, academics, consultants and politicians never spoke or wrote without the catch-phrase '1992'. If the aims of the Single European Act are achieved by 31 December 1992 it will be a miracle and I expect, as with so many EC initiatives over the decades, aspects of it will be rephased or even the 'clock stopped' as in the agricultural crisis of 1965. The decisions taken at Maastricht in December 1991 on political and economic union will, no doubt, change their shape and speed before union is achieved.

Obviously the literature on the EC is vast; the Communities themselves issue nearly 3,000 publications a year and every commercial publisher feels it is politic to have some titles on the EC, but much of this publishing has been sheer duplication. Even publications dealing with specialized subjects tend to devote several chapters to the history and the development of the Communities and to its institutions, sometimes leaving the 'specialized' part only suitable for a long learned article. The aim of this bibliography is to create a list of books published mainly in English for the general reader, combining older publications with the new. Very often the older publications retain something of the history of the development of the EC which gets lost in subsequent editions or newer titles. An attempt has also been made to help the businessman as he grapples with '1992'.

The European Commission have certainly worked hard to see that information about the Communities is available. As the programme to create the Single European Market within the borders of the European Communities (EC) by the end of 1992 comes to fruition and as the two intergovernmental conferences on Political Union and Monetary Union continue their deliberations, the need for information grows. Amongst the key elements of the information policy of the EC structure are the Offices of the European Commission and the European Parliament; the Sales Offices of the Office for Official Publications of European Communities; the Euro Info Centres and the EC Depository Library Network.

Keeping up to date with developments in the EC has become difficult for many of the 13 million small and medium enterprises in the European Community. Many are still unaware of either the challenges or the opportunities that the single market offers to their business. Recognizing this situation, the EC initiated the Euro Info Centre network (EICs) to give European businesses better access to information on EC matters. There are at present 187 centres in the member states of the European Communities: 21 are based in the UK. The EICs act as links to supply companies with information on all aspects of Community affairs, its policies, regulations and prospects. The aim is to provide up-to-date information which is of direct relevance to business. Each EIC operates independently, through various 'host' organizations which have already established close contacts with local firms (Chambers of Commerce, Regional Development Agencies, etc.). Yet each EIC is well integrated into its local business community, experienced in the interpretation and practical application of EC policies, familiar with sources of business advice, and proficient in the use of computerized information retrieval systems.

The EC Depository Library Network is divided into three sections: European Documentation Centres (EDC), Depository Libraries (DEP), and European Reference Centres (ERC). European Documentation Centres comprise substantial collections of the publicly available documentation of the European Communities. There are forty-four EDCs in the United Kingdom mainly in university and polytechnic libraries. Their primary function is to stimulate and sustain the development of the study of Europe in the academic institutions of the region in which they are based. In addition they are requested, when circumstances permit, to provide an EC information service to the wider community. The sort of data which are to be found in an EDC consist of legislation, documentation of the legislative and judicial processes, research studies and reports, statistical titles, explanatory and background documentation.

I should like to thank Tony Holbrook and his staff at Bath University Library, the staff at the European Communities offices in London and Brussels, the London Library and the many publishers I badgered for exact bibliographical data. I have to give particular thanks to Mike Cooper, who was extremely helpful in chasing elusive material; to Ian Thomson for help and on whose *The Documentation of the European Communities* (q.v.) I have leaned heavily for EC publications; to Len Jones for proof-reading and useful comments, to Dione Daffin for help with the index and to Penny White for her painstaking typing of the entries.

John Paxton
1992

Chronology

1946
19 September   Winston Churchill, in a speech at Zürich, urges Franco-German reconciliation with 'a kind of United States of Europe'.

1947
5 June   General George Marshall proposes US aid to stimulate recovery in Europe.
29 October   Creation of Benelux, the economic union of Belgium, Luxembourg and The Netherlands.

1948
16 April   Convention for European Economic Co-operation signed, the birth of the Organization for European Economic Co-operation (OEEC).

1949
5 May   Statute of the Council of Europe signed.

1950
9 May   Robert Schuman makes his proposal to place French and German coal and steel under a common authority.

1951
18 April   The Treaty setting up the European Coal and Steel Community (ECSC) is signed in Paris.

1953
10 February   ECSC common market for coal, iron ore, and scrap begins operations.
1 May   ECSC common market for steel begins operations.

1955

1–3 June

Messina Conference when the Foreign Ministers of the Community's member states propose further steps towards full integration in Europe.

1957

25 March

Signature of the Rome Treaties setting up the EEC (Common Market) and Euratom.

1958

1 January

The Rome Treaties come into force: the EEC and Euratom are established.

19–21 March

First session of the European Parliament; Robert Schuman elected president.

1959

1 January

First tariff reductions and quota enlargements in the Common Market. Establishment of common market for nuclear materials.

20 November

European Free Trade Association (EFTA) Convention signed between Austria, Denmark, Norway, Portugal, Sweden, Switzerland and the UK.

1961

9 July

Greece signs association agreement with the EEC (comes into force 1 November 1962).

1 August

Ireland applies for membership of the EEC.

10 August

The UK and Denmark request negotiations aiming at membership of the Common Market.

8 November

Negotiations with the UK open in Brussels.

15 December

The three neutrals, Austria, Sweden and Switzerland, apply for association with the Common Market.

1962

30 April

Norway requests negotiations for membership of the Common Market.

1963

14 January

President de Gaulle declares that the UK is not ready for Community membership.

29 January

UK negotiations with the Six broken off.

1 July

Signature of the Yaoundé Convention, associating 18 independent states in Africa and Madagascar with the Community for five years from 1 June 1964.

12 September

Turkey signs association agreement with the Community (comes into force 1 December 1964).

1964

9 December First meeting of the Parliamentary Conference of members of the European Parliament and parliamentarians from the Yaoundé-associated states.

15 December Council adopts the Mansholt Plan for common prices for grains.

1965

31 March EEC Commission proposes that, as from 1 July 1967, all Community countries' import duties and levies be paid into the Community budget and that the powers of the European Parliament be increased.

8 April The Six sign a treaty merging the Community Executives.

31 May Common Market Commission publishes the first memorandum proposing lines of Community policy for regional development.

1 July Council fails to reach agreement by the agreed deadline on financing a common farm policy; French boycott of the Community institutions begins a seven-month-long crisis.

26 July Council meets and conducts business without the French representative present.

1966

17 January The foreign ministers of the Six meet in Luxembourg without the Commission present and agree to resume full Community activity.

10 November UK Prime Minister, Harold Wilson, announces plan for 'a high-level approach' to the Six with the intention of entering the EEC.

1967

11 May UK lodges a formal application for membership of the EEC.

1968 UK application for membership of the EEC remains on the table with the Community.

1969

25 April General de Gaulle resigns as President of France.

16 June M. Georges Pompidou elected President of France.

2 December At a summit conference at The Hague the Community formally agrees to open membership negotiations with the UK, Norway, Denmark and Ireland on their applications of 1967.

Chronology

1970

29 June   Talks begin in Luxembourg between the Six and the UK, Norway, Denmark and Ireland.

1971

23 June   Council of Ministers of the Community announces that agreement has been reached with the UK for basis of the accession of the UK to the Communities.

11–13 July   At a Ministerial-level negotiating session, agreement is reached on major outstanding issues: the transitional period for the UK; Commonwealth sugar; capital movements; and the common commercial policy.

28 October   Vote in the House of Commons on the motion 'That this House approves Her Majesty's Government's decision of principle to join the European Communities on the basis of the arrangements which have been negotiated.' The voting figures in the House of Commons were 356 for, 244 against, majority for 112; and in the House of Lords 451 for, 58 against, majority for 393.

1972

22 January   Treaty of Accession signed in Brussels between the European Communities (France, Belgium, Federal Republic of Germany, Italy, Luxembourg and The Netherlands) on the one side and the UK, Denmark, Norway and Ireland on the other side.

22 July   EEC signs free-trade agreements with Austria, Iceland, Portugal, Sweden and Switzerland.

26 September   Rejection by Norway of full membership of the EEC following a referendum.

31 December   UK and Denmark withdraw from EFTA.

1973

1 January   UK, Ireland and Denmark join the Community.

1 April   First 20 per cent cut in industrial tariffs between the original Six and the new member states.

14 May   EEC signs a free-trade agreement with Norway.

1974

1 January   Second 20 per cent cut in tariffs on imports between the UK, Ireland and Denmark and the original Six is made. UK adopts the Common Customs Nomenclature.

1975

28 February   The Lomé Convention, establishing an overall trading and economic co-operation relationship between the EEC and 46 developing African, Caribbean and Pacific (ACP) countries, is signed in Togo.

5 June   UK holds the first referendum and the electorate votes by a two-to-one majority to remain in the EEC.

12 June   Greece applies to accede to the Communities.

1976

April   EEC signs agreements with Maghreb countries (Tunisia, Algeria and Morocco) which guarantee to the 800,000 of their citizens who work within the Community the same working conditions and social security rights as are enjoyed by nationals of Community countries. The agreements also contain important trade, economic, technical and financial co-operation provisions.

1977

January   EEC signs agreements with Mashreq countries (Egypt, Syria, Jordan and Lebanon). These too contain important trade, economic, technical and financial co-operation provisions.

28 March   Portugal applies to accede to the Communities.

28 July   Spain applies to accede to the Communities.

1978

6–7 July   European Council, held in Bremen, decides to institute a European Monetary System (EMS).

1979

9–10 March   European Council, held in Paris, gives the signal for the European Monetary System (EMS) to come into effect. The original starting date, 1 January 1979, had to be abandoned pending agreement on monetary problems in the agricultural sector.

28 May   Greece and Community sign the Treaty of Accession whereby Greece becomes the tenth member with effect from 1 January 1981.

7–10 June   First direct elections in which the voters of the nine member states vote for the 410 members of the European Parliament.

31 October	Community's nine member states sign the second Lomé Convention with their 158 African, Caribbean and Pacific partners.
20 November	Council endorses the results of the Tokyo Round of negotiations within GATT.
29–30 November	Dublin Summit fails to agree to Britain's demand for a reduction in the UK's net contribution to the Community budget.
13 December	European Parliament rejects the 1980 budget.

1980

30 May	Agreement is reached by the Council of Ministers on the problem of the British contributions to the Community budget. It is conceded that while it is not equitable to impose an excessive financial burden on a less prosperous country there will be no ceiling to national contributions.

1981

1 January	Greece becomes the tenth member state of the Communities.

1982

12 August	The European Communities reject a US embargo on the use of US technology for the construction of the Soviet–Western Europe natural gas pipeline.

1984

13 March	EC ministers approve farm reforms which include lowering dairy production quotas, and sanction fines for over-production.
14–17 June	Elections took place for the European Parliament.
27 July	The European Parliament blocks repayment to UK of US$ 600,000,000 although the EC had agreed payment because the UK had to bear an unfair share of the EC budget.

1985

10 September	The foreign ministers of the European Communities approved sanctions against the Republic of South Africa in the hope that this would help to end apartheid.
2–4 December	The first revisions of the Treaty of Rome agreed in the Single European Act which would lead to the lifting of the remaining barriers to trade and commerce among members by 31 December 1992.

1986

1 January | Spain and Portugal become the eleventh and twelfth member states of the European Communities.

16 September | Agreement by the EC to ban new investment in the Republic of South Africa and to ban South African imports of iron, steel and gold coins into Europe.

1989

15 June | Elections took place for the European Parliament.

1990

16 July | Malta applied for full membership of EC.

3 October | The Federal Republic of Germany reunited with the German Democratic Republic; the GDR ceased to exist.

1991

10 December | European leaders in Maastricht agreed treaties on political and economic union, while the British prime minister, John Major, won an opt-out clause on single currency and the removal of the social chapter.

History

Post-war Europe

1 **Postwar: the dawn of today's Europe.**
Richard Mayne.   London: Thames & Hudson, 1983. 336p.
This excellent book sets the scene for all that happened in Europe from the end of
World War II until the establishment of the EEC. Details of major events of these
crucial years are provided, such as the Nuremberg trials, the Marshall Plan, the Berlin
blockade and airlift, Russia's explosion of the atomic bomb, and decolonization. It is
vividly written and it is a good reminder of the great progress and 'miracles' of
reconstruction that took place during the post-war years. There is a very extensive
bibliography. Mr Mayne is the author of the highly regarded *The recovery of Europe*
(1970) (q.v.), a work which was more concerned with the diplomatic process and the
institutional arrangements affecting European integration, whereas this publication
highlights the social and economic change, the impact of science and technology, and
decolonization.

2 **The recovery of Europe: from devastation to unity.**
Richard Mayne.   London: Weidenfeld & Nicolson, 1970, rev. ed. 1973.
375p. bibliog.
Europe in this work is 'western' Europe and is the story of the miracle of change from
rationing to affluence. Mayne's hero in all this is Jean Monnet, the founding father of
the EEC.

European Recovery Program (Marshall Plan)

3 **The origins of the Marshall Plan.**
John Gimbel. Stanford, California: Stanford University Press, 1976. 344p.

In this book Gimbel attempts to demonstrate that the Marshall Plan did not come about as a response to the USSR and that it was not an element of the Cold War, but rather it was a means of making German economic recovery politically acceptable to both Europe and the USA.

4 **The European Recovery Program.**
Seymour E. Harris. Cambridge, Massachusetts: Harvard University Press; London: Oxford University Press, 1948. 309p.

The author aimed to convince the American public of the size of the European post-war economic problems and to warn them that instant recovery and prosperity were not likely.

5 **The Marshall Plan: America, Britain, and the reconstruction of Western Europe, 1947–1952.**
Michael J. Hogan. Cambridge, England: Cambridge University Press, 1987. 544p.

This book presents the fullest account yet written of America's programme to assist Europe after World War II – certainly the most celebrated and successful peacetime foreign policy pursued by the United States in the twentieth century. But, as the author shows, the Marshall Plan was more than an effort to put American aid behind the economic reconstruction of Europe. American officials hoped to refashion Western Europe into a smaller version of the integrated single-market and mixed capitalist economy that existed in the United States. Professor Hogan's emphasis on integration is part of a major reinterpretation that sees the Marshall Plan as an extension of American domestic and foreign-policy developments stretching back through the inter-war period to the progressive era. In this sense, the Marshall Plan becomes the brainchild of the New Deal coalition of progressive private groups and political élites. The book demonstrates that realizing the neo-liberal design required a degree of collaboration between public officials in Washington and between European and American policy-makers that was not always forthcoming. In this context, the author examines the opposition mounted by conservative opponents in Congress, bureaucratic wrangling, and diplomatic obstructionism, particularly by Britain, all of which contributed to a reformulation of American policy. This is an impressive history of the birth and development of the Marshall Plan. It is stronger on the political impact of the Plan than on the economic processes.

6 **Marshall Plan days.**
Charles P. Kindleberger. Boston, Massachusetts: Allen & Unwin, 1987. 273p.

The author worked on the Marshall Plan at the US State Department and this volume consists of fourteen papers written over forty years.

7 **The Marshall Plan and Germany.**
Edited by Charles Maier, Gunter Bischof.   Oxford: Berg, 1991. 464p.

An international team of distinguished political and economic historians provide the definitive analysis of the origins and impact of the Marshall Plan on Germany and on European reconstruction.

8 **Britain and the Marshall Plan.**
Henry Pelling.   London: Macmillan, 1988. 192p.

The Marshall Plan, originally proposed by General Marshall, the US Secretary of State, as a means of providing dollars for the post-war recovery of Europe, operated for the four years 1947 to 1951. In this study, based on both British and American sources (including for the first time the papers of the American 'Mission' in London), Pelling examines the economic relations between the two countries in this period.

9 **The Marshall Plan and its meaning.**
Harry Bayard Price.   New York: Cornell University Press, for Governmental Affairs Institute, 1955. 424p.

The Marshall Plan ended in 1951 and this is a report by the Government Affairs Institute which was commissioned by the US Economic Co-operation Administration to recount the history of the Marshall Plan and to evaluate its achievements.

10 **Plan Marshall.** (The Marshall Plan.)
Jean Teissedre.   Paris: Hermann, 1948. 158p.

A study of the European scene before the Plan was introduced. It includes details of the Plan and good summaries of the main reports.

The Treaties

11 **Treaties establishing the European Communities: as amended by subsequent treaties.**
London: Her Majesty's Stationery Office (Cm 455), 1988. 298p.

The importance of the Single European Act, which entered into force on 1 July 1987 after ratification by twelve member states of the European Community was that it amended the Treaty of Rome to speed up the creation of the single market. This is a consolidated version of the treaties establishing the European Communities as amended by all subsequent treaties including the Single European Act. It contains the Treaty of Paris, setting up the European Coal and Steel Community, and the two Treaties of Rome, setting up the European Economic Community and Euratom.

General books on the birth and development of the Communities

12 **The economics of the European Community.**
Edited by Ali M. El Agraa. Hemel Hempstead, England: Philip Allan, 1990. 3rd ed. 416p.

This comprehensive textbook has been brought fully up to date with new developments in the Community. The first part of the book outlines the historical, institutional and statistical background to the EC, whilst the second discusses customs unions and their impact, and the third considers questions of policy.

13 **A common man's guide to the Common Market.**
Hugh Arbuthnott, Geoffrey Edwards. London: Macmillan, 1989. 2nd ed. 160p.

The purpose of this book is to explain, as clearly as possible, how the policies of the Community are meant to achieve its primary objectives. It is a fully revised and extended version of the book first published in 1979, and is written by two authors who have direct experience of how the Community works.

14 **Europe of many circles: constructing a wider Europe.**
Richard Body. London: New European Publications, 1991. 182p.

This book sets out how the European Community can be reshaped into something big enough to serve the people of all Europe, while also small enough in power to allow her people to enjoy both democracy and individual liberty.

15 **Community Europe: a short guide to the Common Market.**
Roger Broad, Robert Jarrett. London: Oswald Wolff, 1967. 172p.

A good short guide.

16 **The European Community: a guide to the maze.**
Stanley A. Budd, Alun Jones. London: Kogan Page, 1989. 3rd ed. 256p.

This is a simple and useful guide and should be helpful to many who are ignorant about EC matters. It describes the range of Community policies, and the EC's organization and functions, and traces the continuing development of the Community. It especially aims to increase the accessibility of accurate and up-dated information by providing various sources of information about the Community and its workings.

17 **Economic policy for the European Community: the way forward.**
Alec Cairncross, Herbert Giersch, Alexandre Lamfalussy, Giuseppe
Petrilli and Pierre Uri, preface by Herbert Giersch. London:
Macmillan, for the Institut für Weltwirtschaft an der Universität Kiel,
1974. 245p.

In this book five distinguished economists have come together to consider the future of
the European Community and to examine some of the economic problems to be faced
in the future. All aspects of Community policy are considered and new and intriguing
solutions are presented to help solve the slowness of change.

18 **The European Common Market and Free Trade Areas: a progress
report.**
Miriam Camps. Princeton, New Jersey: Center for International
Studies, Princeton University, 1957. 30p.

Provides a succinct account of EEC activity just at the point when the Treaty of Rome
was about to come into force and gives details of last-minute efforts to find a
compromise on the Free Trade Area.

19 **The first year of the European Economic Community.**
Miriam Camps. Princeton, New Jersey: Center for International
Studies, Princeton University, 1958. 28p.

A progress report on the first year of the implementation of the Treaty of Rome which
is extremely useful for its account of the arrangements 'the Six' made with the other
members of the Organization for European Economic Co-operation (OEEC) and with
other institutions such as the General Agreement on Tariffs and Trade (GATT) which
was signed in 1947 by twenty-three countries and directed toward the reduction of
trade barriers.

20 **The politics of the Common Market.**
W. Hartley Clark. Englewood Cliffs, New Jersey; London: Prentice
Hall, 1967. 180p.

A very readable introduction to the Community's political framework.

21 **Economic politics of the Common Market.**
Edited by Peter Coffey. London: Macmillan, 1979. 212p.

In its eight chapters on agricultural, industrial, social, fiscal, trade and monetary,
transport, regional, and energy policies, this book examines these important areas of
economic policy of the European Community. There is a basic theoretical introduction
to each policy area, followed by a description of what constitutes Community policy in
each case.

22 **Basic problems of the European Community.**
Edited by P. D. Dagtoglou. Oxford: Blackwell, 1975. 304p.

The articles in this volume queried whether the European Community was going to
survive as an integrated or integrating unit, or whether it was going to recede towards a
simple free trade area. This is a collection of major German contributions and gives
insight into continental reasoning in 1975.

5

23 **Europe without frontiers.**
Edited by Piet Dankert, Ad Kooyman. London: Cassell, 1989. 118p.
In this book socialist leaders from European Community countries – Neil Kinnock, Willy Claes, Laurent Fabius, Felipe González, Wim Kok, Hans Jochen Vogel and Jacques Delors – examine the current state of social democracy in their countries and discuss its rôle in the future development of an integrated Europe. They address common problems and preoccupations – disappointing economic growth, unemployment, government budget deficits, stagnant industrial investment, the threat of a new wave of poverty, widening regional disparities, and environmental problems – and propose a joint EC industrial policy based on respect for individual freedom.

24 **The Common Market.**
J. F. Deniau. London: Barrie & Rockcliff and Pall Mall Press, 1960. 139p.
An early overall study of the EEC which explains the implications of the Treaty of Rome. Deniau was the director in charge of EEC relations with Third World countries and the book is an interesting study by a dedicated European.

25 **The Schuman Plan: a study in economic cooperation 1950–1959.**
William Diebold, Jr. New York: Praeger, for the Council on Foreign Relations; London: Oxford University Press, 1959. 750p. map.
A detailed study of the policies and success of the European Coal and Steel Community (ECSC) during the transitional period between 1953 and 1958. Its strength is that it is written for students of economics and international affairs and also for those engaged in the steel industry.

26 **The European perspective, the formative years. The struggle to establish the Common Market and the Political Union (1958–66).**
Hans von der Groeben, preface by Sir Con O'Neill. Luxembourg: Office of Official Publications of the European Communities, 1987. 276p.
Dr von der Groeben helped to draft the Treaty of Rome and was a member of the EEC Commission. This study analyses the success of economic integration and the failure of the efforts to move towards political union in the period 1958–66. This work was originally published in 1982 by Nomos Verlagsgesellschaft, Baden-Baden as *Aufbaujahre der Europäischen Gemeinschaft – Das Ringen um den Gemeinsamen Markt und die Politische Union (1958–66).*

27 **The uniting of Europe: political, social and economical forces 1950–1957.**
Ernst B. Haas. London: Stevens, for the London Institute of World Affairs, 1958. 552p.
The establishment of the European Coal and Steel Community became the blueprint for the study of European unity. At the time of this publication, it was the only supra-national body which had functioned. Haas believed that the supra-national technique was the best way of establishing unity and was much more effective than the inter-government methods of such organizations as the Organization for European Economic Co-operation (OEEC), the forerunner of the Organization for European Co-operation and Development (OECD).

28   **The European Community: a new path to peaceful union.**
     Walter Hallstein.   New York: Asia Publishing House, for the Indian
     Council for Cultural Relations, 1964. 72p. (Azad Memorial Lectures
     1963).
Two lectures given by the president of the EEC dealing with internal aspects of the
Common Market and the place of a united Europe in the world. He also gives his
views on the relationship between the Community and the under-developed world.

29   **United Europe: challenge and opportunity.**
     Walter Hallstein.   Cambridge, Massachusetts: Harvard University
     Press; London: Oxford University Press, 1962. 109p. bibliog.
These three lectures were given by the then President of the European Commission to
the Fletcher School of Law and Diplomacy of Tufts University. Wholly committed to
the success of the EEC, he gives his views of the rôle of the 'Eurocrat'. In no way is it
a critical study of the workings of the EEC.

30   **The European Economic Community: a policy for reform.**
     Neil Hamilton.   London: Institute of Directors, 1983. 64p.
This pamphlet, giving the views of the Institute of Directors, pinpoints the areas within
the EC needing reform in the early 1980s. It covers taxation, customs and transport
procedures, documentation, technical barriers, standardization, state aids, monopolis-
tic and restructuring practices in private firms, and there is an appendix listing
recommendations.

31   **The political economy of integration in the European Community.**
     Jeffrey Harrop.   Aldershot, England: Edward Elgar, 1989. 224p.
This book provides detailed coverage of the key areas of economic activity. Each
chapter follows a common format: the reader is first introduced to the issues involved
and then presented with an in-depth analysis of the process and consequences of
Community economic integration in major areas – trade (both within the Community
and with the outside world), agriculture, regional development, monetary and fiscal
integration and industrial policy. The concluding section discusses the effects of
sectoral integration on the United Kingdom.

32   **Understanding attitudes to the European Community: a social-
     psychological study in four member states.**
     Miles Hewstone.   Cambridge, England: Cambridge University Press,
     1986. 306p.
This monograph deals with attitudes to the European Community in Britain, France,
Germany and Italy. Hewstone's questionnaire was answered by 545 university students
and he aimed to discover what they knew, thought and felt about the European
Community. Feeling without knowing seems to have dominated. The common
agricultural policy (CAP) and bureaucracy seemed to come top of the list of dislikes.

33 **European Community economics.**

T. Hitiris.   Hemel Hempstead, England: Harvester Wheatsheaf, 1991.
2nd ed. 336p.

This is a completely revised and up-dated version of a very successful textbook. The
first edition, published in 1988, was somewhat of a misnomer as it concentrated on the
institutions of the EC; this aspect has been improved. The European Community has
undergone rapid changes in recent years not least because of the 1992 initiative. The
programme to complete the single market has fostered other, new initiatives towards
greater co-operation, integration and union of the Community's nations – a social
charter for people's rights, monetary integration and even political union are on the
agenda. World events have also had a major effect on the Community and its policies –
notably the rapid political changes in Eastern Europe and the Uruguay Round of
General Agreement on Tariffs and Trade (GATT) negotiations. All of these changes
and events have been incorporated in the new edition. In addition, there is a
substantially increased treatment of the analytical issues for assessing the problems of
economic integration, notably the theoretical foundations and underpinning integration, the welfare effects of the single market, and the basic theory of economic policy.

34 **Economic divergence in the European Community.**

Michael Hodges, William Wallace.   London: Allen & Unwin, for the
Royal Institute of International Affairs, 1981. 227p.

Some early observations on the need to get the European Community moving again
following the establishment of the common external tariff, the European Coal and
Steel Community and the common agricultural policy. Much space is devoted to
exchange rate policy and the authors examine some of the decisions to be taken in the
1990s. These observations anticipate many of the topics raised in the Single European
Market debate.

35 **Europe under stress: convergence and divergence in the European
Community.**

Yao-su Hu.   London: Butterworths, for the Royal Institute of
International Affairs, 1981. 120p.

The second half of this book is the more interesting. The author takes various aspects
of policy – agriculture, external commercial relations, the European Monetary System
(EMS) and the Community budget – and gives a refreshing insight into the success or
failure of each of these. There are some interesting views on the economic strength of
the Federal Republic of Germany and its implications for the Community. The author
also makes the novel suggestion that political integration should precede economic
integration.

36 **The futures of Europe.**

Edited by Wayland Kennet.   Cambridge, England: Cambridge
University Press, for the Commission of the European Community,
1976. 242p.

Wayland Kennet was the director of the 'Europe plus Thirty' project which was
instigated by Professor Dahrendorf when he was an EEC commissioner. Dahrendorf
was worried that there was no central forecasting instrument and he wondered
whether, if there was such an instrument, it should be institutionalized. *The futures of
Europe* is the revised and partly rewritten report of this investigation.

37 **The Common Market and how it works.**
Anthony J. C. Kerr. New York; Oxford: Pergamon Press. 3rd ed.
1986. 316p. bibliog.
One of the best English-language introductions to the enlarged European Community.
After a general introduction and historical background, essential details of the member
states are presented, followed by a description of the Community's institutions and
decision-making processes. Kerr then succinctly explains the Common Agricultural and
Fisheries policies, the Rules of Competition, and the social and regional policies of the
Community. There are also details about industry and technology, coal and steel, the
environment, energy and transport.

38 **The challenge of the Common Market.**
Uwe Kitzinger. Oxford: Blackwell, 1962. 174p.
An early analysis aiming 'to describe the Community which we [Britain] are now
seeking to enter and to emphasise to a wider public those trends on the Continent
which the government, by its own confession, came to understand too late'. The author
succeeds in explaining how and why the European Communities came about, and
elucidates the commitments under the Treaties and the practical application. There is
an excellent chapter on supra-nationalism and sovereignty which is still pertinent in the
1990s.

39 **The European Common Market and Community.**
Edited by Uwe Kitzinger. London: Routledge & Kegan Paul, 1967.
226p.
Mainly extracts from twenty-four of the important documents dating from July 1944
and relating to European integration.

40 **The Schuman Plan.**
Bernard Lavergne. Paris: Presses Universitaires de France, 1951. 111p.
This is an attack on the Schuman Plan. It discusses lucidly the uncertainties felt by
many in France, and elsewhere, at this period in the development of European history,
and it argues for an Atlantic union rather than a 'Third Force'.

41 **The European Community and the challenge of the future.**
Edited by Juliet Lodge. London: Pinter, 1989. 334p. bibliog.
This survey of the European Community provides details of developments in its
institutions and policies, both internal and external, over the last decade. It is stronger
on the recent past than on predictions for the future.

42 **The Belgium–Luxembourg Economic Union, 1921–39: lessons from an early experiment.**
James E. Meade. Princeton, New Jersey: International Finance Section, Department of Economics and Sociology, Princeton University, 1956. 41p.

Professor Meade believes that a common currency is essential for a successful economic union. He declares that the Belgium–Luxembourg Economic Union of the inter-war period was successful because there was a large and a small partner, and because both countries adopted a common currency, namely, the Belgian franc.

43 **Negotiations for Benelux: an annotated chronicle 1943–56.**
James E. Meade. Princeton, New Jersey: International Finance Section, Department of Economics and Sociology, Princeton University, 1957. 89p.

The negotiations to establish Benelux exposed many of the problems which were later encountered in establishing the EEC, including trade in agricultural products and balance-of-payments disequilibrium. Professor Meade used original documents to produce this extremely valuable chronicle.

44 **Creating the European Community.**
R. W. Mowat, with a foreword by Jean Rey. London: Blandford, 1973. 235p. bibliog.

This clear and succinct account of what Mowat calls 'the *re*integration of a fragmented Europe of the interwar years' takes the story as far as the autumn of 1972.

45 **The European Communities in the 1990s: economy, politics and defence.**
Brian Nelson, David Roberts, Walter Viet. Oxford: Berg, 1991. 256p.

An examination of the key issues facing the European Communities in the 1990s: the politics of integration, economy, education and science, and foreign policy and defence.

46 **Understanding the European Communities.**
William Nicoll, Trevor C. Salmon. Hemel Hempstead, England: Philip Allan, 1990. 265p.

This book is written at a level accessible to those approaching the often complex subject matter for the first time. The text examines in depth the nature and rôle of the Community's institutions, their relationship with one another, and their involvement in the decision-making process. It also looks at other issues, including the nature of the budgetary system and important policy areas such as the Common Agricultural Policy (CAP) and external relations.

47 **A political geography of Community Europe.**
Geoffrey Parker. Borough Green, England: Butterworths, 1983. 141p.

The objective of this book is to unravel the extent to which Community Europe has acquired its own distinctive geopolitical characteristics. It examines the factors which have brought about the emergence of the European Communities. There is an interesting chapter on the three Euro-capitals: Brussels, Luxembourg and Strasbourg,

History. General books on the birth and development of the Communities

but a large part of the book is given over to the external dimensions of Community Europe. It looks at whether the EEC is a potential superpower and the likelihood of its achieving an international importance comparable with that of the United States and the Soviet Union.

48   **Landmarks in European unity.**
Edited by S. Patijn, introduction by Henri Brugmans.   Leyden, The Netherlands: Sijthoff, 1970. 223p.

A collection of twenty-two documents on European unity. They consist of excerpts from official papers, speeches, communiqués, excerpts from press conferences, printed in English and French, and range from 1946 (Churchill's speech at Zürich) to 1969 (The Hague Summit).

49   **The developing Common Market.**
John Paxton.   London: Macmillan, 1976. 3rd rev. ed. 240p.

A general, straightforward guide to the Common Market. The first edition of this book, *Structure and development of the Common Market*, was published by Hutchinson in 1968 and the second edition, *Into Europe*, was published in 1972 also by Hutchinson. Useful for the student, it contains much which might now be called 'redundant' history of the EEC, but which is no longer available elsewhere.

50   **European Community: the building of a union.**
John Pinder.   Oxford: Oxford University Press, 1991. 256p.

This book details how the transformation of relations among member states has resulted from a series of steps: the strengthening of the Community's institutions; its enlargement from six to twelve; the moves from customs union to the single market and from the European Monetary System (EMS) to the project for economic and monetary union; and the development of agricultural, budgetary, industrial, social, and foreign policies. After constructing a complete and coherent view of the Community, the author assesses the political and economic forces for and against unification. He squarely confronts the question of whether the Community is likely to become a federal state, and offers his own neo-federalist approach.

51   **La Communauté Européenne du charbon et de l'acier.** (The European Coal and Steel Community.)
Paul Reuter, with a preface by Robert Schuman.   Paris: Librairie Général de Droit et de Jurisprudence, 1953. 320p. bibliog.

This is an invaluable scientific guide to the problems with which the High Authority (now the Commission) was confronted in 1953. It is conveniently divided into 308 sections and cross-referenced throughout. More up to date is *Coal, steel and the rebirth of Europe, 1918–1955: the Germans and French from Ruhr conflict to Economic Community* by John Gillingham (Cambridge, England: Cambridge University Press, 1991. 336p.), the first large-scale historical investigation of the critical first stage of European integration, the creation of the European Coal and Steel Community (ECSC). The author discusses the thirty-year Franco-German struggle for heavy industry mastery in Western Europe, describes the dreams and schemes of Jean Monnet, who designed the heavy industry pool, reveals the American vision that inspired the work, and discloses how his transatlantic partners used their great authority to assure its completion. He also lays bare the operating mechanisms of the coal–steel pool, showing that contrary to the hopes of Monnet and his supporters, the ECSC restored rather than reformed the European economy, leaving an industry still dominated by the giant producers of the Ruhr.

52 Unite or perish: a dynamic program for a United Europe.

Paul Reynaud, introduction by William J. Donovon.   New York: Simon & Schuster, 1951. 214p.

Reynaud, a distinguished French statesman and one of the creators of the Council of Europe, describes the many elements which eventually led to the creation of the EEC. These include the Marshall Plan and the Organization for European Economic Co-operation, the European Payments Union, and the Schuman and Pleven Plans. The work is prefaced by a plea for a revival of the European tradition and European spirit.

53 The European Community fact book.

Alex Roney.   London: Kogan Page, 1989. 187p.

The convenient question-and-answer format of this fact book is divided into sections which cover how the European Community works – its aims, size and structure; the policies and developing areas of influence of the Commission; business strategy and how business is affected by the overall economic and social plan of the Community.

54 From free trade to integration in Western Europe?

Christopher Saunders.   London: Chatham House and PEP, 1975. 107p.

Saunders begins with the premise that there was in 1974 almost free trade in industrial goods, and then goes on to consider what is needed to move towards greater integration. He argues that the Common Agricultural Policy will form some sort of protection from high world prices and urges greater trade links with Eastern Europe. He also sees the need for a movement towards a greater degree of integrated production between EEC member countries, but calls for some protection in sensitive areas such as aircraft, computer and agricultural production – in other words, a continental division of labour.

55 The path to European union: from the Marshall Plan to the Common Market.

Hans A. Schmitt, with a foreword by W. Walton Butterworth.   Baton Rouge, Louisiana: Louisiana State University Press, 1962. 272p. bibliog.

This is a detailed study of the workings of the European Coal and Steel Community which acted as a pilot scheme for the EEC. Only published material has been used as Schmitt had no access to inside archives.

56 How can Europe survive?

Hans F. Sennholz.   New York: Van Nostrand; London: Macmillan, 1955. 336p.

An interesting study, by an American, of European plans for European unity. He concludes that all plans are hopeless because 'the majority of Europeans believe in socialism and the welfare state. And all European governments are committed to policies of interference with businesses'. In view of the powers of the EC as we move towards 1992 this book is worth re-reading.

57 Europe: journey to an unknown destination.

Andrew Shonfield.   London: Allen Lane, 1973. 96p.

An expanded version of the BBC Reith Lectures for 1972 in which the author examined the many problems faced by member countries of the EEC coming together to act as a powerful force in the world.

58 Perspectives in Europe.

Edited by Edward A. Stettner.   Cambridge, Massachusetts: Scheukman, 1970. 191p.

An edited account of a symposium held at Wellesley College, Massachusetts, USA in the spring of 1969. There were four parts and the second dealt with EEC matters and economic affairs. There was no British representative speaking at this session which discussed Britain's possible entry to the EEC, and the consensus seemed to be that the advantages of joining were doubtful.

59 Making sense of Europe.

Christopher Tugendhat.   London: Viking, 1986. 239p.

Tugendhat draws on his experience as a British Member of Parliament and on his eight years as a member of the European Commission, four of which he spent as a vice-president of the Commission. The Europe referred to in the title is, of course, the European Community. The author provides practical guidelines for changes that are to come, such as the creation of a single market by 1992, and his writings on European defence are pertinent. He sees a still-expanding European Community that would always remain a beneficent complement to, and not a substitute for the individual states.

60 The transformation of Western Europe.

William Wallace.   London: Pinter, for the Royal Institute of International Affairs, 1990. 122p.

A much-needed study, written in an easy style, on the political, social and economic changes that have taken place since 1945. The author is particularly good at explaining how the EC was reactivated into the concept of 1992 and beyond. *From Luxembourg to Maastricht: 100 critical days to Europe* by Stanley Crossick, Max Kohnstamm and John Palmer (Brussels: Belmont Europe Policy Centre, 1991. 156p.) poses further questions and attempts some answers. It contains an analysis of critical issues facing the Community in 1991–92 (including the August 1991 events in the Soviet Union), the EC agenda until end 1991, the full text, summary and analysis of the new Treaty of the Union, and spells out the scale of the challenges facing the Community. It argues that further enlargement of the Community to twenty or more member states is now inevitable, and that such an enlargement will demand ever deeper integration: 'Any attempt to restrict the Community to a privileged club would be a betrayal of the basic ideals and objectives which inspired its foundation'. The authors propose some concrete ways of preparing for a new European Treaty in 1995. They suggest that both the European Commission and the European Parliament, together with the national parliaments of the member states, should be invited to help prepare for the review stipulated in the draft treaty provisions on political union.

61 **The European Common Market: growth and patterns of trade and production.**
Ingo Walter.   New York: Praeger, 1967; London: Pall Mall, 1968. 212p.
A preliminary study of the growth of EEC trade for the period 1953–65.

62 **The European Community in the 1970s.**
Edited by Steven Joshua Warnecke.   New York: Praeger; London: Pall Mall, 1972. 228p.

A collection of papers presented to a conference at City University of New York in October 1971. Its main value lies in the discussion on the Community's relations with the United States. William Diebold suggests in one paper that the unity of Europe is useful, even when it hurts the United States and that 'an integrated Europe should be able to help more effectively than a divided one in managing the international economic system'. Other contributors are Ralf Dahrendorf, Harald Malmgren, Andrew Pierre, Louis Jaquet, Gordon Adams and Uwe Kitzinger.

63 **The European Community: establishment and growth.**
New York: Charles Scribner's Sons, 1975. 208p. maps.

Although dated 1975, this research report retains a considerable amount of useful information which tends to get lost in more modern publications, and therefore it is of value to the historian. It is based on information contained in *Keesing's Contemporary Archives* (see item no. 622).

64 **The European Community: past, present and future.**
Journal of Common Market Studies, vol. 21, no. 1–2 (Sept.–Dec. 1982), 244p.

This important collection of essays, marking twenty years of the journal, comprises a wide range of contributions from academics from EC member states and beyond. Topics covered include the politics of Community building, the rôle of the nation-state, external policy and the EC, and the mobility of labour and capital. Writing before the launch of Lord Cockfield's White Paper renewed popular enthusiasm for integration, the editor – Loukas Tsoukalis – is able to strike a pessimistic note, feeling that there was then a real danger of the EC becoming 'an irrelevance with no real value'.

65 **The new Europe.**
London: European Parliamentary Labour Party, 1990. 18p.

A statement from the European Parliamentary Labour Party explaining why they consider that Labour is the only political party with a clear vision of the new Europe which moves forward dramatically with '1992'.

66 **Pocket guide to the European Community.**
Foreword by Roy Jenkins.   London: Economist Books, 1989. rev. ed. 192p.

This guide sets out the origins, the ideals and ambitions, the institutions, problems and arguments that have moulded the European Community into the organization we know today.

Biographies

General

67   **Dod's European Companion 1991.**
London: Dod's Publishing and Research, 1991. 2nd ed. 700p.
This directory contains 1,500 biographical entries, with photographs of senior civil servants and politicians in the member states, Council of Ministers, the Commission, Parliament, the Court of Justice, European Investment Bank, and other key institutions. It also explains how European legislation is made and examines the structure of the various institutions. In addition it has addresses, telephone and telex numbers, abbreviations and a glossary.

68   **Who's Who – European Communities and other European organisations, 1991–92.**
Brussels: Editions Delta, 1991. 4th ed. 460p.
The biographical complement to the *Yearbook of the European Communities and of other European organisations* (q.v.) this Who's Who includes the biographies of the senior civil servants working within the European Communities and within more than twenty other European organizations such as Council of Europe, Eurocontrol, European Patent Office, etc. Also included are the members of the permanent representations and heads of mission accredited to the European Communities, the chairmen and secretaries of the non-governmental European organizations and of the professional organizations set up at Community level. It is trilingual in French, English and German.

Biographies. Leading personalities

69　**Who's Who in European politics, 1990–1991.**
　　Editorial Advisory Board: Lord Jenkins, Simone Veil, Martin
　　Bangemann.　Sevenoaks, England: Bowker-Saur, 1990. 781p.
There are over 6,000 biographies of politicians at all levels of twenty-two countries (EC
plus EFTA plus Turkey, Cyprus and Malta), plus membership of the European
Parliament and Commission. The second part of this Who's Who is a comprehensive
political directory by country, with details of all key posts and their holders. Mailing
address, phone and fax numbers are included for all key posts.

Leading personalities

Callaghan

70　**Time and chance.**
　　James Callaghan.　London: Collins, 1987. 584p.
This autobiography is of particular interest for his views on Europe and the problems
he faced during his period in Government and Opposition.

71　**Callaghan: the road to Number Ten.**
　　Peter Kellner, Christopher Hitchens.　London: Cassell, 1976. 187p.
One chapter in this book stands out: '1974–6 Common Market Odyssey'. It deals with
the renegotiation of Britain's terms of membership of the EC and the referendum, the
first ever in Britain, when Callaghan was foreign secretary.

de Gaulle

72　**Charles de Gaulle.**
　　Don Cook.　London: Secker & Warburg, 1984. 432p.
This publication is particularly good at explaining the de Gaulle concept of Europe,
from the Atlantic to the Urals, and his attitude towards Britain's membership. We are
reminded of his pronouncement 'One day the British will join the Common Market,
but I will not be around to see it'.

73　**De Gaulle: a political biography.**
　　Alexander Werth.　Harmondsworth, England: Penguin, 1965. 391p.
An excellent political biography giving details of de Gaulle's tendency always to rebel
against something. His concept of a future Europe is explained and analysed. *De*

16

Gaulle: the ruler 1945–1970 by Jean Laconture (London: Collins Harvill, 1991. 640p.) is an excellently translated second volume of an outstanding biography by the foreign editor of *Le Monde* and deals very adequately with de Gaulle's attitude to Britain, the EC, the USA and non-EC Europe.

Macmillan

74 Harold Macmillan.
Nigel Fisher.   London: Weidenfeld & Nicolson, 1982. 220p.
Two chapters in this book, 'Macmillan and Europe' and 'The French veto', are particularly good. They give an insight into Macmillan's mind and the influence of his experience in the First World War on his approach to European affairs.

75 At the end of the day.
Harold Macmillan.   London: Macmillan, 1973. 555p.
Several chapters of this, the sixth volume of autobiography by Harold Macmillan, cover the period from July 1961 – when the British Cabinet agreed that the government should make a formal application to accede to the Treaty of Rome – until January 1963 – when de Gaulle vetoed United Kingdom's entry.

Marjolin

76 Robert Marjolin: architect of European unity, memoirs 1911–1986.
Translated by William Hall, foreword by Eric Roll, preface to the French edition by Raymond Barre.   London: Weidenfeld & Nicolson, 1989. 458p.
Marjolin was the first secretary-general of the Organization for European Economic Co-operation (OEEC), later the Organization for European Economic Cooperation and Development (OECD). His co-operation with Jean Monnet helped to produce the first post-war economic plan. He negotiated the Treaty of Rome in 1957 and became a vice-president of the Commission of the European Economic Community (EEC) in 1958.

Marshall

77 General Marshall: a study in loyalties.
Robert Payne.   London: Heinemann, 1952. 335p.
This interesting biography gives an insight into the thinking and actions of the man who was responsible for the inspiring post-war lifeline, the Marshall Plan.

Monnet

78   **Jean Monnet and the United States of Europe.**
Merry Bromberger, Serge Bromberger, translated by Elaine P.
Halperin.   New York: Coward-McCann, 1969. 349p.

A somewhat gossipy account of Jean Monnet's drive towards European integration, aimed at an American audience.

79   **Jean Monnet, a grand design for Europe.**
P. Fontaine.   Brussels: Commission of the European Communities,
1988. 51p.

This booklet was published to mark the centenary of the birth of Jean Monnet, a founding father of the European Community. It explains his philosophy and principles for Europe.

80   **Memoirs.**
Jean Monnet, translated by Richard Mayne, foreword by Roy Jenkins.
London: Collins, 1978. 554p.

The long public career of Jean Monnet extended back to the First World War when he helped to co-ordinate the British and French economic war effort. The Monnet Plan later became the Schuman Plan for the pooling of Western Europe's coal and steel industries, and the chapters dealing with the birth and development of the plan are of considerable interest.

Schuman

81   **Robert Schuman: homme d'Etat, 1886–1963.** (Robert Schuman:
statesman, 1886–1963).
Robert Schuman.   Paris: Imprimerie Nationale, 1986. 520p.

This volume of memoirs throws light on Robert Schuman, the French statesman who founded the European Coal and Steel Community (ECSC) and who looked forward to a 'United States of Europe'. It also gives us additional information on the European Coal and Steel Community (ECSC), the European Defence Community and the decolonization of France. A valuable contribution to the history of the post-World War II era.

Spaak

82   **Mr Europe: a political biography of Paul Henri Spaak.**
    J. H. Huizinga.   London: Weidenfeld & Nicolson, 1961. 248p.
A good portrait of the greatest Belgian statesman of his generation, but slightly
inadequate in that Mr Spaak's early life and the Belgian royal crisis are very well
covered while more attention could have been given to the most dynamic part of his
career: his part in establishing Benelux, his diplomatic attempts to encourage The
Netherlands to sign the Brussels treaty, and his great patience with France following
that country's rejection of the European Defence Community.

Truman

83   **The Truman administration: principles and practice.**
    Edited by Louis W. Koenig.   New York: New York University Press,
    1956. 394p.
President Truman, the 33rd president of the USA, had much involvement with
Europe. This included supporting his secretary of state in the US-sponsored European
Recovery Program, better known as the Marshall Plan, and denying that the Plan was
imperialist as the USSR complained.

Wilson

84   **The politics of Harold Wilson.**
    Paul Foot.   London: Penguin, 1968. 347p.
In this book there is a chapter 'America, Commonwealth or Common Market' and,
although not favouring Wilson's pragmatic approach to these issues, it gives an insight
into the problems facing the then Prime Minister.

Jean Monnet Lectures

85   **The Single Act and Europe, a moment of truth.**
Jacques Delors.   Luxembourg: Office for Official Publications of the
European Communities, 1988. 40p.

This Jean Monnet Lecture was given in Florence at the tenth anniversary of the
opening of the European University Institute in 1986. For most years since 1977 a
distinguished statesman, academic or public figure has been asked to give the Jean
Monnet Lecture in memory of one of the key figures in the history of the integration
process in Europe. Other lectures include: *Europe: present challenge and future
opportunity* by Roy Jenkins (1977); *Appointments for Europe* by Emilio Colombo
(1978); *A Third Europe* by Ralf Dahrendorf (1979); *The Community and European
identity* by Simone Veil (1980); *Jean Monnet: the power of the imagination* by Max
Kohnstamm (1981); *Towards the European Union* by Altiero Spinelli (1983);
European Union or decline: to be or not to be by Gaston Thorn (1984); *European
Union: one character in search of an author* by Giulio Andreotti (1985); *Europe from
the Community of Twelve to European Union: the objective for 1992* by Felipe
González Marquez (1987).

Member States

General

86   **Unity with diversity in the European economy: the Community's southern frontier.**
Edited by Christopher Bliss, Jorge Braga de Macedo.   Cambridge, England: Cambridge University Press, for the Centre for Economic Policy Research, 1990. 368p.
Presents a detailed account of the problems facing Greece, Spain and Portugal as they become more integrated with the EC.

87   **Six European states: the countries of the European Community and their political systems.**
Stephen Holt.   London: Hamish Hamilton, 1970. 414p. bibliog.
A straightforward study of the political systems of the Six, i.e. the original members of the EEC: Belgium, France, the Federal Republic of Germany, Italy, Luxembourg and The Netherlands. Excellent footnotes and bibliographies are included.

88   **Collision in Brussels: the Common Market crisis of 30 June 1965.**
John Newhouse.   London: Faber & Faber, 1968. 195p.
A balanced view of the de Gaulle versus the EEC Commission row. The disagreements arose from an opinion of the EEC Commission that a new budget procedure would be a step towards full budgetary powers for the European Parliament. These proposals were totally rejected by France, and the French government withdrew its representatives from the Commission's committees. Agreement on a new scheme, known as the Luxembourg Agreement, was eventually reached in January 1966.

89   **France, Germany and Europe.**
     Haig Simonian. *Journal of Common Market Studies*, vol. 19, no. 3
     (March 1981), p. 203–20.
The Franco-German axis has long been a pillar of the EC. In an extensive review of
the relationship during the 1960s and 1970s the author concludes that although much
will depend on individual ministries and personalities, strong institutional links – seen
by Jean Monnet as the key to integration – will mean that the two powers will continue
to work closely together.

90   **Building Europe: Britain's partners in the EEC.**
     Carol Twitchett, Kenneth J. Twitchett.   London: Europa, 1981. 254p.
     bibliog.
This is a book for students and most of the illustrative examples date from 1975–80.
Each chapter gives details, with a member country's approach to the EC. Considerable
space is also given to the first direct elections to the European Parliament in 1979.

France

91   **Socialists and European integration: a study of the French Socialist Party.**
     Byron Criddle.   London: Routledge & Kegan Paul; New York:
     Humanities Press, 1969. 116p.
A lively account of the Party's attitude and policy towards integration from 1945 to
1969. Socialist ideology seems to have played a minor rôle, with the anti-Communist
and anti-a-united-Germany sentiments being dominant.

Germany

92   **The Federal Republic of Germany and the European Community.**
     Simon Bulmer, William Paterson.   London: Allen & Unwin, 1987.
     288p.
The Federal Republic of Germany (FRG) is the strongest national economy within the
European Community. Over the past two decades, as the historical burden of the Nazi
era has receded, the FRG has also become an increasingly important political force in
the EC. The authors examine governmental policy over the period 1969–86 and explain
this in terms of the political, economic and administrative dynamics of the Federal
Republic. The study includes analyses of the attitudes and the rôle of West German
interest groups, political parties, public opinion, the legislative and the federal states
regarding European policy. The impact of Franco–German and German–German
relations on European policy is also considered.

93 **West Germany's role in the European Community – some speculation on future trends.**
Gisela Hendriks. *European Access*, 1900, 2 (April), p. 10–12.
An article written before the reunification of Germany in 1990, but containing a useful analysis of Germany's attitude to the EC and its aim for closer economic and political ties with Eastern Europe.

94 **Federal Republic of Germany and EC membership evaluated.**
C. C. Schweitzer, D. Karsten. London: Pinter, 1990. 279p.
This book was written before the reunification of Germany, but it is nevertheless valuable in that it studies the gains and losses to Germany of membership of the EC. The editors feel that, on balance, Germany has gained. There is a useful discussion on the relationship of the individual *Länder* (Federal states) with Brussels.

95 **The Federal Republic of Germany and the European Community: the presidency and beyond. (Reports given at the symposium held at the College of Europe, Bruges, 5–7 November 1987).**
Edited by Wolfgang Wessels, Elfriede Regelsberger. Bonn: Europe Union Verlag, 1988. 328p.
A collection of papers given to a symposium in November 1987 and dealing with 'the interests and responsibilities of the Federal Republic of Germany within the European Community and in the overall integration process'.

Greece

96 **The EC and the Greece–Turkey dispute.**
Panos Tsakaloyannis. *Journal of Common Market Studies*, vol. 19, no. 1 (Sept. 1980), p. 35–45.
The long-standing enmity between Greece and Turkey, focusing on Cyprus, has long been seen as a potential barrier to Turkey's EC membership. Written after Greece's application for membership of the EC had been approved, but before accession itself, this article examines the EC's attitude to the Cypriot question, with a detailed account of EC–Cypriot–Greece–Turkey relations from the 1950s. Interestingly, in the light of Turkey's renewed interest in membership, Tsakaloyannis argues that Turkey's attempts to join the Community are more likely to be frustrated by her inability to meet the EC's own criteria for membership than by Greek diplomacy.

97 **Greece and the European Community.**
Edited by Loukas Tsoukalis. Farnborough, England: Saxon House, 1979. 172p.
This volume records a conference on 'Greece and the European Community' held in September 1977. The conference papers have been supplemented by others specially commissioned in order to produce the work under review. The conference members included diplomats, members of the negotiating teams, academics and journalists. The

majority of the papers (and comments on the papers) in this volume are by academics and deal with the history of the negotiations for Greek entry into the EEC, the likely economic effects of entry on both Greece and the EEC, and the broader context of the Greece–EEC relationship.

98 **Main legal problems arising during the interim period and immediately after Greece's accession to the EC.**
Xenophon A. Yalaganas. *Journal of Common Market Studies*, vol. 20, no. 4 (June 1982), p. 333–59.
A detailed treatment of the troubled domestic background to the start of Greek membership. The author examines the use of the EC card in domestic party politics, Greek 'guerrilla diplomacy', and the internal debate surrounding membership. He concludes that in many ways Greece could ill afford the systematic contravention of EC rules that at the time seemed a possibility.

99 **Greece and the European Community: the first decade of a troubled association.**
G, N. Yannapoulos. London: Sage, 1975. 35p.
This essay was written just as Greece was applying for full membership of the European Community. It details the Community's reaction to the military régime but Yannapoulos concludes that 'once a degree of market interdependence among nations reaches a critical point it makes their relationship one that often transcends and bypasses political preferences'.

Ireland

100 **Irish industry and 1992: what has Ireland gained from membership of the European Community and what are the issues that concern it most as the magic date of 31 December 1992 approaches?**
Liam Connellan. *European Access*, 1989, 5 (October), p. 10–12.
An article full of confidence for the future of Ireland within the EC, written by the director-general of the Confederation of Irish Industry. He believes that too much emphasis has been placed on the peripheral location of the Republic.

101 **Ireland and the European Communities: ten years of membership.**
Edited by David Coombes. Dublin: Gill & Macmillan, 1983. 202p.
Ireland's experience as a member of the European Community holds the clue to how the Community has functioned over the last ten years. As one of the smaller and economically weaker members, Ireland has tested economic policies of the Community in a particularly rigorous fashion. Ireland, as an important agricultural producer, has seen many of the benefits of the Common Agricultural Policy. An interesting study emphasizing the view that Ireland has a desire to achieve non-market-driven 'single Europe' after 1992, with the slogan 'Keep economics out of agriculture' can be found in *The single European market and the Irish economy*, edited by Anthony Foley and Michael Mulreany (Dublin: Institute of Public Administration, 1990. 500p.).

102   **The tortuous path: the course of Ireland's entry into the EEC 1948–73.**
      D. J. Maher, foreword by P. J. Hillery.   Dublin: Institute of Public
      Administration, 1986. 419p.

Chronicles the events which led up to the entry of Ireland into the EEC in 1973. It
starts with the economic development of the Irish state from 1922 and follows through
to 'the path leading tortuously but inexorably to increased Irish involvement in
European affairs'.

103   **Northern Ireland and Irish integration: the role of the European
      Community.**
      Seamus O'Cleireacain.   *Journal of Common Market Studies*, vol. 22,
      no. 2 (Dec. 1983), p. 107–24.

An examination of the relationships between Belfast, London, Dublin and the EC in
the 1970s and 1980s. The author suggests that the EC may have a rôle in giving
London a way out of the situation as both North and South benefit from greater
economic convergence, and as the economic barriers to a unified Ireland begin to fall.
Dublin can benefit from integration with Ulster without being seen to make political
capital out of the situation.

104   **Ireland: a neutral in the Community.**
      Trevor Salmon.   *Journal of Common Market Studies*, vol. 20, no. 3
      (March 1982), p. 205–29.

Despite affirmed neutrality, Ireland is a well-established member of an international
organization. In a detailed analysis of Irish–EC relations Salmon points out the internal
contradictions in this relationship which, he argues, will become increasingly
problematical. Despite the lack of formal arrangements, Ireland is being pulled into
European defence because it is impossible in practice to separate many questions of
international economics and trade from politics and defence. Closer co-operation with
her European partners will inevitably mean co-operation on areas impinging upon
defence and 'it appears to be increasingly difficult to reconcile neutrality with
Community membership'.

Italy

105   **Italy's approach to the EC.**
      Geoffrey Pridham.   *Journal of Common Market Studies*, vol. 19, no. 1
      (Sept. 1980), p. 74–83.

An examination of a selection of Italian political and academic literature on the
country's relations with the EC, drawing mainly on material from the 1970s. The
author finds strong interest in the EC, particularly in the political aspects of European
union, but, disappointingly, is unable to find any clear pointers to the real heart of
Italian thinking about the Community.

106 **Italy chooses Europe.**
F. Roy Willis.   London; New York: Oxford University Press, 1971.
373p. bibliog.
The economic and political history of Italy from the decision to accept Marshall Aid after World War II to full membership of the EEC. The Common Market economic miracle convinced the doubters that there were serious advantages in EEC membership.

107 **Italy since 1945.**
Elizabeth Wiskemann.   London: Macmillan; New York: St Martin's
Press, 1971. 142p. bibliog.
A short, well-written general book on post-war Italy, emphasizing the pace of change – especially in customs and ways of life – up to 1971. Wiskemann devotes two chapters to economic recovery and membership of the EEC.

Spain

108 **Customs union enlargement and adjustment: Spain's accession to the**
EC.
Robert C. Hine.   *Journal of Common Market Studies*, vol. 28, no. 1
(Sept. 1989), p. 1–28.
The author examines the theory behind enlargement of customs unions and compares Spanish experience to this model. He finds that as specialization between member states has not developed as expected, agricultural trade is, and will continue to be, a problem. The Single Market may only increase Spain's adjustment problems.

109 **Spain to 1992: joining Europe's mainstream.**
Mark Hudson, Stan Rudcenko.   London: Economist Intelligence
Unit, 1988. 114p.
This report offers a clearly presented projection of likely trends. Spain's entry to the European Community in 1986 represented one of the important aspects of its socialist government's objectives for modernization. Spain has been a leading advocate of the Single Market in 1992 and for the drive towards European unity.

110 **Spain, the EEC and NATO.**
Paul Preston, Denis Smyth.   London: Routledge & Kegan Paul, for
the Royal Institute of International Affairs, 1984. 96p.
An analysis of the political factors which had to be faced by Spain before joining the EEC and NATO. Nearly half the book is devoted to the transition to democracy between 1973 and 1984.

United Kingdom

111 Commonwealth or Europe.
   G. St. J. Barclay.   St Lucia, Queensland, Australia: University of
   Queensland Press, 1970. 210p. bibliog. (The Commonwealth: Problems
   and Perspectives).
Barclay believed that Britain should choose Europe rather than the Commonwealth
and in this study looks at the attitudes of Britain and the major Commonwealth
countries to this problem.

112 Is there any choice? Britain must join Europe.
   Edward Beddington-Behrens.   Harmondsworth, England: Penguin,
   1966. 141p.
Beddington-Behrens was pro Europe but against supra-nationalism. He writes that
EEC is 'like all voluntary associations of States, based on consent'. He was against
direct elections to the European Parliament but wanted more control over European
spending.

113 The General says no: Britain's exclusion from Europe.
   Nora Beloff.   Harmondsworth, England: Penguin, 1963. 181p.
A good general introduction to British relations with continental Europe, including a
detailed study of Britain's negotiations to join the EEC.

114 Britain and the European Community 1955–1963.
   Miriam Camps.   Princeton, New Jersey: Princeton University Press;
   London: Oxford University Press, 1964. 547p.
An enormously detailed description of this volatile period in Britain's approach to the
Community. Half the book deals with the establishment of the new Europe, of
Britain's first attempt to come to terms with the proposal of a free trade area and the
creation of EFTA (the European Free Trade Association). The second half deals with
the period from 1960 to the beginning of the government's change of heart. The
writing is a mixture of official documents, news reports and interpretations by the
press, plus the author's interviews with civil servants and others close to the scene of
action.

115 The case against joining the Common Market.
   Paul Einzig.   London: Macmillan; New York: St Martin's Press, 1971.
   132p.
This book gives the opposite picture to those who think that there is nothing but good
in the Common Market, but it is unlikely to convince anybody except those who have
already decided 'against'.

116 De Gaulle's Europe or why the general says no.
Lord Gladwyn. London: Secker & Warburg, 1969. 168p.

Lord Gladwyn held views diametrically opposed to those of President de Gaulle and believed that the nation-state is an out-dated political concept. He shows that de Gaulle was looking for an independent rôle for France in European affairs, and a self-reliant Europe under French leadership, with the Federal Republic of Germany as the main partner.

117 The challenge of Europe: can Britain win?
Michael Heseltine. London: Weidenfeld & Nicolson, 1989. 226p.

Michael Heseltine, a UK Conservative cabinet minister, offers some exciting new ideas to the European debate, including setting up an upper house for the European Parliament. He presses for more research and development, particularly in the UK. He stresses the UK's interdependency and questions the concept of sovereignty. The book is a little short on historical perspective.

118 Britain and Europe: ten years of Community membership.
Roy Jenkins. *International Affairs*, vol. 59, no. 1 (Winter 1982–83), p. 147–53.

Roy Jenkins was President of the European Commission 1977–81 and in this article he states that for too long the question of 'in or out?' has absorbed British politicians to the neglect of what Britain should do *in* Europe. This is a succinct appraisal of the activity, or lack of activity, in the first ten years of Britain's membership of the Community. He ends the article with the words: 'The deep economic and social problems Britain faces can only be solved by the British themselves. But the EEC can provide the stability in foreign policy and the strength and security in economic policy which I believe are the vital basis for the regeneration and renewal of Britain.'

119 Britain and the EEC.
Edited by Roy Jenkins. London: Macmillan, 1983. 249p.

A series of essays which assess the impact of British membership of the EC on its economic and political institutions. They originated as lectures given at the meeting of the British Association for the Advancement of Science in 1982. John Marsh and Christopher Tugendhat write on agriculture, John Pinder and Roger Morgan write on political institutions, Geoffrey E. Wood considers money, Francis Cripps looks at macroeconomic policy, Geoffrey Denton writes on the regions, Robert Grant on industry, Martin Wolf on trade and David Wall on the EEC and the Third World. The book contains an account by F. S. Northedge of past relations between Britain and the EEC. It also includes an important essay by the editor on Britain, the EEC and the future.

120 Economics: Britain and the EEC.
Harry G. Johnson. London: Longmans, 1969. 111p.

This collection of papers, read at a symposium in February 1969 at the University of Ghent, cogently explains the financial and monetary implications and particularly the Sterling Area, competition and price policy, and budgetary problems of Britain's membership of the EEC.

121 **Diplomacy and persuasion: how Britain joined the Common Market.**
Uwe Kitzinger. London: Thames & Hudson, 1973. 432p.
A lucid study of the long road travelled by Britain before joining the Communities. It includes much detail of the British parliamentary debates in 1971 and 1972.

122 **The second try: Labour and the E.E.C.**
Edited by Uwe Kitzinger. Oxford: Pergamon Press, 1968. 353p. bibliog.
This is a useful and well-selected set of documents to illustrate the Labour Party's attitude towards the European Economic Community. It ranges from 1950, when UK Prime Minister Clement Attlee gave his views on the Schuman Plan in the House of Commons, to the veto by President de Gaulle of France at the end of 1967.

123 **Towards one Europe.**
Stuart de la Mahotière. Harmondsworth, England: Penguin, 1970. 332p.
The aim of this book is to marshal a considerable body of facts to help British readers to come to conclusions on the rights and wrongs of EEC membership.

124 **The community of Europe.**
Richard Mayne. London: Gollancz, 1962. 192p.
An enthusiastic attempt to encourage British membership of the EEC and 'a brief history of a great movement'.

125 **Britain faces Europe 1957–1967.**
Robert L. Pfalzgraff, Jr. Philadelphia, Pennsylvania: University of Philadelphia Press; London: Oxford University Press, 1969. 228p. bibliog.
A highly documented study of Britain's evolving relationship with the Common Market in the period 1957–67.

126 **Britain and Europe – how much has changed?**
William Pickles. Oxford: Blackwell, 1967. 119p.
A restatement of the familiar case against British membership of the Community. Pickles believes that EEC bureaucracy must lead to federalism and he searches for an alternative, including a grouping of the Commonwealth, USA and the European Free Trade Association (EFTA).

127 **Britain and the Common Market.**
John Pinder. London: Cresset, 1961. 134p.
This book, written for the layman rather than the expert, describes the nature of the European Economic Community and its achievements, at a time when Britain was deciding whether or not to join. Arguments are advanced against joining, the political and economic benefits to be gained from being part of the process of European integration, and the dangers of standing aside.

128 **Problems of British entry into the EEC: reports of the Action Committee of the United States of Europe.**
Edward Pisani, foreword by Kenneth Younger, John Pinder. London: Chatham House and PEP, 1969. 108p. (European Series, no. 11).
An excellent survey of the problems faced by Britain at the time of her decision to join the EEC.

129 **La Grande Bretagne et la Communauté Européene.** (Great Britain and the European Community.)
Françoise de la Serre. Paris: Presses Universitaires de France, 1987. 224p.
An account of Britain's belated entry into the Community and its somewhat pragmatic approach to co-operation. Its eight chapters, arranged chronologically, are dominated by economic matters although the great political debates are well reported. The questions of whether the Community has altered Britain or whether Britain has altered the Community are well documented and an even-handed appraisal is given. The volume covers the period to 1986 – when Britain accepted the Single European Act – and the author expresses optimism about the rôle of Britain in the Community.

130 **Britain and new Europe: the future of the Common Market.**
Michael Shanks, John Lambert. London: Chatto & Windus, 1962. 253p. bibliog.
The usual summary of the aims and institutions of the EEC, with cogent arguments in favour of Britain's membership.

131 **European reckoning: the Six and Britain's future.**
E. Strauss. London: Allen & Unwin, 1962. 177p.
A well-argued case against Britain's entry of the EEC. The then held belief that membership of EEC would solve all Britain's ills is exploded.

132 **Terms of entry: Britain's negotiation with the European Community 1970–1972.**
Simon Z. Young. London: Heinemann, 1973. 220p.
A useful handbook dealing with the long negotiations for British entry. It is not always clear why or how compromise was reached on some issues. The author concludes that the UK's future within the Community will depend on 'the general condition of international life in Western Europe and the world, and only in part on the terms of entry'.

Enlargements of the EC

133 A wider European Community? Issues and problems of further enlargement.
Geoffrey Edwards, William Wallace.   London: Federal Trust for Education and Research, 1976. 83p.

The authors argue that the enlargement of the Community will be its crucial test and conclude that 'Further enlargement may mark the end of the road begun in Messina in 1955. Alternatively, it may force the existing members to face up to those awkward choices between different paths towards European unity which have in recent years been so determinedly evaded'.

134 The politics of the European Community.
Roy Pryce.   London: Butterworth, for the Centre for Contemporary European Studies, 1973. 209p.

This volume looks at the changes that an enlargement would bring to the development and functioning of the Community. The prolonged negotiations on this issue of enlargement caused many unforeseen issues to emerge.

135 The enlargement of the European Community.
Edited by José Luis Sampredo, Juan Antonio Payno.   London: Macmillan, 1983. 288p.

A study of the likely economic, social and political impact of membership of the EEC of Greece, Portugal and Spain.

136 The second enlargement of the EEC: the integration of unequal partners.
Edited by Dudley Seers, Constantine Vaitsos with Marja-Liisa Kiljunen.   London: Macmillan, 1982. 275p.

This book is in a series of works investigating the issues posed by the planned second enlargement of the European Community to embrace, after Greece, Spain and Portugal. In this volume enlargement is assessed in terms of the anticipated impact it may have on the structure of Western Europe, the Common Agricultural Policy (CAP), the European Monetary System (EMS), industry and the European Community's poor regions – the Maghreb, Mashreq, African, Caribbean and Pacific (ACP) countries, and the newly industrializing states of Asia.

137 The European Community's Mediterranean policy after the second enlargement.
Françoise de la Serre.   *Journal of Common Market Studies*, vol. 19, no. 4 (June 1981), p. 377–87.

Writing at the time of Greece's accession to the Community, the author examines the likely consequences of this enlargement and the possible entry of Spain and Portugal for EC policy in the Mediterranean region. She finds a lack of co-ordinated policy and argues that enlargement will result in less financial support for non-member states in the region, and that the EC will be drawn into regional disputes such as those over Cyprus or the Western Sahara, the Arab–Israeli dispute, and Balkan politics.

138 **The European adventure: tasks for the enlarged Community.**
Altiero Spinelli.   London: Charles Knight, 1972. 194p.

Spinelli, a member of the Commission and founder of the European Federal Movement in Italy, gives a round-up of his thinking for the medium- and long-term future of the Communities. He is constructive on such matters as monetary policy with the need for the *écu* as the unit of account and as an intervention currency. He also gives his views on regional policy and on the Common Agricultural Policy (CAP), but he realizes that little progress will be made as long as 'politically speaking, the Community . . . is mute and headless'.

139 **The European Community and its Mediterranean enlargement.**
Loukas Tsoukalis.   London: Allen & Unwin, 1981. 273p.

The aims of the book are to provide details of the political and economic issues raised by the entry of Greece, Spain and Portugal into the Community and – in the second part – to analyse the consequence to the Community of further enlargement. The author believes that insufficient debate about enlargement policy has taken place.

140 **A Community of Twelve? The impact of further enlargement on the European Communities.**
Edited by William Wallace, I. Herreman.   Bruges, Belgium: De Tempel, 1978. 442p.

This volume, containing papers submitted at a conference held in Bruges in 1978, is useful because it adds to our understanding of the problems involved and the implications for Community institutions and policies, as well as for the three applicant countries, Greece, Portugal and Spain. Members of the conference were politicians, officials and academics from the Nine (the original Six members – Belgium, France, Germany, Italy, Luxembourg, The Netherlands – plus Denmark, Ireland and the UK) and the Three. The first part of the book contains the speeches made by official representatives from the Nine and the Three but the major section of the book discusses the legal and institutional aspects of enlargement. A useful study of European integration.

141 **Customs unions and trade conflicts: the enlargement of the European Community.**
G. N. Yannopoulos.   London: Routledge, 1988. 184p.

A straightforward analysis of the impact of the expansion of the EC on trade. The author suggests that if chicken and pasta wars are to remain minor lapses in EC–US relations, the speeding up and strengthening of General Agreement on Tariffs and Trade (GATT) procedures would be an ideal way to reduce commercial tensions.

The Institutions of the Communities

General works: the decision-making process

142 **Democratising the Community.**
Vernon Bogdanor.   London: Federal Trust for Education and
Research, 1990. 20p.
In this discussion paper the author argues that if the Community is not made more
relevant and accountable to the European electorate, there is a real danger of
widespread disenchantment with its institutions, and that will lead to stagnation in the
integration process. He goes on to state that the Community needs a stronger, more
dynamic, democratic executive than the Commission and it needs a Commission acting
as a presidential executive, independent of Parliament, directly elected and party-
based, which would develop sufficient legitimacy and leadership to give expression to a
genuine European identity. He also suggests that European-wide referenda on major
issues would add to its legitimacy and effectiveness.

143 **Domestic politics and EC policy making.**
Simon Bulmer.   *Journal of Common Market Studies*, vol. 21, no. 4
(June 1983), p. 349–64.
An examination of the interaction of national political entities with the European
entity. The author discusses the rôle of national governments in the EC, their domestic
political environments, and the structures and attitudes that lie behind policy-making.

144 **The European Council: decision-making in European politics.**
Simon Bulmer, Wolfgang Wessels.   London: Macmillan, 1987. 174p.
In December 1974 the Heads of Government of the nine member countries agreed to
meet, accompanied by the Ministers of Foreign Affairs, three times a year. These
meetings have become known as the European Council (which should not be confused

The Institutions of the Communities. The decision-making process

with the Council of Ministers or the Council of Europe). The authors state that 'the Community's history since 1975 is the history of summit meetings' and claim that the European Council is 'the most politically authoritative institution' (although technically not an institution). This is an excellent guide for those who want to know how this body came into existence and what its achievements are.

145   **Politics and bureaucracy in the European Community: a portrait of the Commission of the EEC.**
       David Coombes.   London: Political and Economic Planning (PEP) and Allen & Unwin, 1970. 343p.

Coombes considers how far the process of European economic and political integration can be achieved with the institutions established by the Treaty of Rome. He believes that the objective cannot be realized because the Commission has failed in its political rôle.

146   **The institutional framework of the European Communities.**
       D. A. C. Freestone, J. S. Davidson.   London: Routledge, 1988. 256p.

A concise introduction to the institutions and law-making processes of the Community, setting them in their proper perspective as part of UK public law.

147   **Politics and policy in the European Community.**
       Stephen George.   Oxford: Clarendon Press, 1985. 205p.

The fundamental question posed by this book is: 'Why have more common Community policies not emerged?' George explains the successes and the more frequent failures of the EC in its attempts to formulate common policies. The second half of the volume considers six areas where attempts have been made to formulate common Community policies: energy, agriculture, economic and monetary affairs, regional policy, enlargement of the Community, and external affairs.

148   **Power and decision in Europe: the political institutions of the European Community.**
       Stanley Henig.   London: Europotentials, 1980. 156p.

A straightforward introductory student text, with a particularly good chapter on the Court of Justice.

149   **Inter-governmental relations in the European Community.**
       C. Hull, R. A. W. Rhodes.   Farnborough, England: Saxon House, 1977. 87p.

The book describes the co-operation (or lack of co-operation) by local and regional authorities with the European Community. Up to 1977, Britain's local authorities do not seem to have responded adequately.

150 **The role of interest groups in the European Community.**
Emil Kirchner, Konrad Schwaiger.   Aldershot, England: Gower,
1981. 178p.
Contains information on links between interest groups and the Commission, European
Parliament and the Economic and Social Committee. It is a useful study of those
groups that exert influence on EC policy-making.

151 **Institutions and policies of the European Community.**
Edited by Juliet Lodge.   London: Pinter, 1983. 264p.
A textbook designed for undergraduates and the general public as an introduction to
the decision-making processes in all aspects of the Communities.

152 **The institutions of the European Community.**
Richard Mayne.   London: Chatham House and PEP, 1968. 82p.
bibliog.
Most of this pamphlet is devoted to a factual survey of Community institutions, but
Mayne's views of changes likely to take place in the rôle of the Council and
Commission are also aired.

153 **Les Groupes de pression dans la Communauté Européene, 1958–1968.**
(Pressure groups in the European Community, 1958–68.)
Jean Meynaud, Dusan Sidjanski.   Brussels: Editions de l'Institut de
Sociologie, 1971.
A study of a number of groups formed with the express purpose of influencing
decisions in matters arising from the existence or actions of the European
Communities. It has pertinent warnings about the need for new dimensions from such
groups as trade unions, consumers, farmers, and professional organizations.

154 **Working together: the institutions of the European Communities.**
Emile Noël.   Luxembourg: Office for Official Publications of the
European Communities, 1988. 47p.
This booklet, by the former secretary-general of the EC Commission, describes
Europe's institutional mechanisms and provides basic information on the *modus
operandi* of the institutions of the European Communities.

155 **The EEC: national parliaments in community decision-making.**
Michael Niblock.   London: Chatham House and PEP, 1971. 112p.
A succinct book on the rôle of national parliaments in the process of decision-making
in the European Economic Community. Niblock explains the limitations, and
acknowledges that after the ratification of the Treaty of Rome and amendments, the
enlargement of the Community, and when debates have taken place on trade and
association agreements, many other Community decisions require no action by
national parliaments. Most of the excitement has been in the EEC budget debates.

The Institutions of the Communities. The decision-making process

156 **Government and politics in the European Community.**
Neill Nugent. London: Macmillan, 1989. 368p.
This textbook on the European Community is divided into three sections. The first examines the origins and historical development of the Community; the second describes the powers, influence, and methods of functioning of the principal Community institutions and political actors; and the third reviews the Community's policy interests and policy processes. Particular attention is given to the fact that there are now few policy areas with which the Community is not in some way involved.

157 **The men behind the decisions: cases in European policy-making.**
Glenda Goldstone Rosenthal. Lexington, Massachusetts; Farnborough, England: Heath, 1975. 166p.
This study, written before the first enlargement of the Community, takes five cases of decision-making: the introduction of the generalized preferences scheme; the conclusion of the association agreement with Morocco and Tunisia; the struggle to achieve free movement of labour; the Mansholt plan on agriculture; and the Werner plan for economic and monetary union. Professor Rosenthal shows the influence of pressure groups in decision-making.

158 **Presenting your case to Europe.**
Peter Danton de Rouffignac. London: Golden Arrow, 1991. 208p.
Companies and organizations are increasingly finding a need to present their case more effectively to the various Community institutions. This applies equally to those wishing to influence the course of European legislation, to apply for Community funding, to attract investment to their city or region, or simply to put across the viewpoint of a trade organization or pressure group. In each case there is a need for a sound knowledge of how the Community works, where and when important information is available to the outsider, where the power really lies, and what can be done to influence the European decision-making process. This book provides a step-by-step guide to the European Community institutions, and shows how policy decisions are arrived at and funds allocated. It examines how national governments monitor Community legislation, and provides a number of case-studies showing how powerful organizations representing employers, trade unions or special interests carry out their lobbying role. A final section includes an 'A to Z' of lobbying techniques that will help any organization present its case more effectively to the politicians and bureaucrats. The *Directory of pressure groups in the European Community*, edited by Alan Butt Philip (Harlow, England: Longman, 1991. 380p.) could also be useful. It is a listing of several hundred lobby groups and associations operating at European Community level. It gives background analysis and commentary on the operations of each group, and for each major pressure group there are full contact details and data on structure, funding, activities, achievements and an assessment of the group's influence. To ensure there is no need to look elsewhere for information, there is an informed overview of how such groups go about their activities, with listings of relevant EC and governmental organizations.

159 **Decision making in the European Community.**
Christopher Sasse, Edouard Poullet, David Coombes, Gérard Deprez. New York: Praeger, for the European Community Institute for University Studies, 1977. 352p.
This book is more concerned with the apparatus of institutional action and is divided into three main parts each of which could stand as a separate publication. The first, by Sasse, deals with the participation of national parliaments and governments in a

proposal for the improvement of the rôle of the Council of Ministers. Poullet and Deprez produce some thought-provoking data on the bureaucracy of the EEC Commission, while the final study analyses the legality of Community decision-making.

160   **Decision-making speed in the EC.**
      Thomas Sloot, Piet Verschuren. *Journal of Common Market Studies*, vol. 29, no. 1 (Sept. 1990), p. 75–85.
An unusual quantitative approach to EC policy-making which refutes much of the 'conventional wisdom' about the ponderous nature of EC bureaucracy. Whilst the authors acknowledge that time delays are present they find that they are getting shorter; they argue that the rate at which new legislation is adopted is quickening; and they find that there is little real evidence to support a popular view of the EC institutions as in a state of permanent crisis.

161   **National governments and European communities.**
      Helen Wallace.   London: PEP and Chatham House, 1973. 104p.
This valuable work analyses what the rôle of national governments should be in the bureaucratic machinery in Brussels. She says '. . . governments are elected to make national policy and to protect national interests, and as yet national goals are not sufficiently identified with Community collaboration for a shared Community interest to be easily defined'.

162   **Policy-making in the European Community.**
      Edited by Helen Wallace, William Wallace, Carole Webb.
      Chichester, England; New York: John Wiley, 1st ed. 1977, 2nd ed. 1983. 360p.
This is the revised, up-dated and extended edition of a standard work on the European Community which examines the range and diversity of Community activity. There are nine chapters, containing case-studies of policy-making for money, competition, industry, regions, energy, sugar, foreign policy, tax, and harmonization. In addition each of the three editors has contributed a chapter on Community policy-making in general.

European Coal and Steel Community

163   **The European Coal and Steel Community: experiment in supranationalism.**
      Henry L. Mason.   The Hague: Martinus Nijhoff; London: Batsford, 1955. 153p. bibliog.
An important study of the first 'community', which at the time of publication, provided clues to the complexities which would follow with the formation of the EEC. It is a well-documented study of the establishment of the ECSC and of its achievements in the first two years of its operation.

Financial report of the European Coal and Steel Community.
See item no. 590.

Investment in the Community coalmining and iron and steel industries.
See item no. 592.

Council of Ministers and the Presidency

164 **Changing the guard in Brussels: an insider's view of the EC presidency.**
Guy de Bassompierre. Washington, DC: Center for Strategic and
International Studies (The Washington Papers), 1988. 162p.

A study of the daily activities of the Council of Ministers of the EC. The author uses
the presidency as a vehicle for examining EC institutions and he consistently links this
to the workings of the presidency, but the depth of appraisal comes in anecdotal
references and explanations which relate to the wider context. The author concludes
with a chapter on US–EC relations and an outlook on future developments. He
advocates that the United States encourage European integration in ways beneficial to
US interests. 'Rather than resist greater European integration . . . it should take up
the challenge of dealing with a closer union of the Twelve, urging it down paths
congenial to US interests.'

165 **The Council of Ministers of the European Community and the President-
in-Office.**
Geoffrey Edwards, Helen Wallace. London: Federal Trust for
Education and Research, 1977. 102p.

This excellent example of institutional analysis examines the idea that the Presidency
of the Council of Ministers of the European Community has achieved a position of
considerable institutional importance, and has made an identifiable impact on
Community decisions.

166 **The presidency of the European Council of Ministers: impacts and
implications for national governments.**
Edited by Colm O'Nuallain. London: Croom Helm, 1985. 300p.

This is a useful book in that it throws light on the presidency and on EC structures for
policy-making. It was a project arranged by the European Institute of Public
Administration in Maastricht. There are some basic snags: there is no index; some
chapters are in French; and some of those in English are obviously not written by a
native speaker.

Review of the work of the Council of Ministers.
See item no. 594.

European Parliament

167 **Your parliament in Europe: the European Parliament 1979–1989.**
George Clark. London: UK Information Office of the European
Parliament, 1989. 60p.

George Clark, a former political correspondent and later European political correspondent of *The Times*, believes that the important rôle of the European Parliament is still largely unknown to the general public and often misrepresented in the media. This booklet is an attempt to redress the balance.

168   The European Parliament: structure, procedure and practice.
Sir Barnett Cocks.   London: HMSO, 1973. 336p.

A guide to the origins, structure, external relations and procedures of the European Parliament compiled by the Clerk of the British House of Commons. There is an appendix giving procedures of the Parliament.

169   The future of the European Parliament.
David Coombes.   London: Policy Studies Institute, 1979. 136p.

The author looks at the various options available for the future of the European Parliament but does not attempt to define what that future should be. He draws on a large number of sources and presents his arguments clearly.

170   Testing the new procedures: the European Parliament's first experience of its Single Act powers.
Richard Corbett.   *Journal of Common Market Studies*, vol. 27, no. 4 (June 1989), p. 359–71.

The author argues that the Single Act has not met the European Parliament's hopes for a new rôle in EC decision-making, although Parliament will take advantage of its new powers and will continue to press for further reform. He concludes that, despite changes for the better, the powers delegated to the EC by its members' parliaments are not subject to true democratic accountability. The article examines the working of the assent and co-operation procedures, and by so doing gives some insight into the powers of the parliaments. Consideration is also given to the Commission's executive powers and the European Parliament's rôle in European political co-operation.

171   One parliament for twelve.
Foreword by Enrique Baron Crespo.   London: European Parliament Information Office, 1989. 11th ed. 20p.

A useful pamphlet which succinctly describes the workings of the European Parliament and lists all the UK members with their party-political affiliations.

172   The European Parliament.
John Fitzmaurice.   Farnborough, England: Saxon House, 1978. 182p.

In the 1970s the rôle of the European Parliament was vague and ill-defined and most books of the period reflect this position. This one is no exception but it is nevertheless a useful work. The author is at his best when describing procedures, committees and parties.

173   The European Parliament and the European Community.
Valentine Herman, Juliet Lodge.   London: Macmillan, 1978. 199p.

A competent and straightforward attempt to explain the European Parliament's rôle up to 1978.

174 **The European Parliament.**
Francis Jacobs, Richard Corbett.   Harlow, England: Longman, 1990.
320p.

This practical source gives you all you need to know about this institution and covers how the Parliament is elected, where it meets, when and using what language, the political groups, leadership structures, the parliamentary committees and delegations, the Parliament as a forum and channel for communication, plenary sessions, the parliamentary secretariat, the Parliament and legislation, the budgetary rôle, scrutiny and control, the Parliament and constitutional change, details of the European elections and a list of Members of the European Parliament (MEPs).

175 **The European Parliament: performance and prospects.**
Emil J. Kirchner.   Aldershot, England: Gower, 1984. 170p.

Kirchner's book is based on research by graduate students at Essex University into the background of the members and their activities in the first three years of the first directly elected European Parliament. It has weaknesses in that it does not investigate the work in committees, where, as in most parliaments, considerable activity takes place; great noise in the chamber is not always an indication of success. The general public are vague about the rôle of members, and although this book does not adequately answer such questions, it could be the basis for further, more detailed study.

176 **A Parliament for the People's Europe of the 1990s?**
Juliet Lodge.   *European Access*, 1990, 1 (February), p. 9–10.

An excellent analysis of the progress made in recent times to strengthen the rôle of the European Parliament. The author also takes a look into the changing Europe of the future.

177 **The European Parliament: what it is – what it does – how it works.**
Michael Palmer.   Oxford: Pergamon, 1981. 235p.

A concise guide to the European Parliament written by its director-general. The most interesting chapters deal with the anomalies created by the different national voting systems, and how members of the European Parliament go about their business.

178 **The European Parliament in the EC policy process.**
Ann Robinson, Adrian Webb.   London: Policy Studies Institute, 1985.
60p.

This is the report of a conference held at Wiston House, Sussex, England, 12–14 October 1984. It took place just as the Parliament entered its second directly elected term of office. It concentrated on the process of debating, enacting and implementing Community legislation and studied these processes from the viewpoint of MEPs past and present, of officials in other Community institutions, of representatives of national political parties and interest groups, and of observers from the research community and the media.

179   **The public image of the European Parliament.**
       Edited by Ann Robinson, Caroline Bray.   London: Policy Studies
       Institute, 1986. 77p.
This study explains that the Parliament's poor public image in the UK is a by-product
of the European Community's overall unpopularity, and that public apathy arises from
the Parliament's ambiguous rôle. It is suggested that a change in attitude can come
about only through a change by national parties and national leaders.

180   **The European Parliament: the three-decade search for a united Europe.**
       Paula Scalingi.   London: Aldwych, 1980. 221p. bibliog.
A book about the efforts made since 1945 to establish a European Parliament in
Western Europe, by direct, universal suffrage. It is particularly good on the failure of
member governments of the EEC to allow direct elections before 1979.

181   **The Times guide to the European Parliament 1989.**
       Alan Wood.   London: Times Books, 1989. 288p.
This guide is published after each European election, and this edition has the results of
the June 1989 elections. It gives a complete, up-to-date analysis of the way the
members of the European Parliament were elected, how the Parliament works and the
power groupings within it; details of voting in the twelve member states, campaigns in
the UK and Europe. The book contains a list of all Euro-MPs in alphabetical order,
giving member state, political group, photograph, address and phone number, and a
biography. Also it lists members of all committees, and there are, in addition,
biographies of members of the EC Commission.

182   **Building a democratic community: the role of the European Parliament.**
       World Today, vol. 45, no. 7 (July 1989), p. 112–17.
This is the text of the second Lothian Memorial Lecture given at Chatham House on
16 May 1989 in which Lord Plumb argues strongly for greater powers for the European
Parliament.

183   **European Parliament list of members.**
       London: Her Majesty's Stationery Office, 1990. 275p.
This directory lists the names, party affiliations and addresses of all members of the
European Parliament.

184   **The Parliament of the European Community.**
       London: Political and Economic Planning, 1964. 119p.
The pamphlet recognizes the importance of the European Parliament. It compares it
with other European parliamentary assemblies, such as the Council of Europe, and
emphasizes the essential difference that the European Parliament is the first
international parliamentary body which is specifically representative of the peoples of
the member states and not of their governments. There is discussion of the need for
giving the Parliament greater powers, the limits laid down by the Treaty of Rome and
the attitude of member states, especially France, to a more powerful parliament.

185 **Ten years that changed Europe, 1979–1989.**
Luxembourg: European Parliament, 1989. 76p.
The period covered by this publication is from when the European Parliament was first elected by universal suffrage to the advent of the Single European Act. It has some excellent statistical material and is a useful reference tool. Naturally, it advocates more power for the Parliament and political union.

Official Handbook of the European Parliament.
See item no. 596.

Rules of procedure.
See item no. 597.

European Parliamentary elections

186 **European elections by direct suffrage: a comparative study of the electoral systems used in western Europe and their utility for the direct election of a European parliament.**
Wolfgang Birke.   Leyden, The Netherlands: A. W. Sijthoff, 1961. 124p. bibliog.
The Rome treaty made clear that a direct suffrage system for the European Parliament was essential. Wolfgang Birke has investigated the alternative electoral systems of the various Western European countries and has shown which systems would be most appropriate for European elections. This work is not in the category of easy reading.

187 **Communicating with voters: television in the first European parliamentary elections.**
Edited by Jay G. Blumler.   London: Sage, 1983. 387p.
Although this collection of essays was published five years after the first European parliamentary elections its findings still remain relevant and supplement other studies on the same subject. The first Euro-elections were unique in that there was considerable public ignorance about the Community which could be offset only by a media-based information campaign.

188 **The first European elections: a handbook and guide.**
Chris Cook, Mary Francis.   London: Macmillan, 1979. 193p.
The first general elections for the European Parliament were a milestone in the evolution and development of political Europe and this book offers some useful analysis on the debate over electoral systems and representations.

189 **Candidates for Europe: the British experience.**
Martin Holland.   Aldershot, England: Gower, 1986. 218p.
A survey of the recruitment and selection process of British candidates for the 1979 European elections. It is particularly well researched because it studies the candidates selected, those rejected, and then goes on to study those actually elected.

190 Direct elections to the European Parliament 1984.
Edited by Juliet Lodge. London: Macmillan, 1986. 287p.
This is a survey of the background, campaign and results of the 1984 European election
of the then ten member states. There is an explanation of the election procedures
adopted and of the reasons for their adoption. It would appear that in each member
state (Denmark being an exception) the election was fought overwhelmingly on
national issues. The editor argues that the election did little to advance understanding
of European problems, especially those dealing with EC institutions – something that
was also true of the British referendum on EC membership.

191 The 1989 election to the European Parliament.
Edited by Juliet Lodge. London: Macmillan, 1990. 249p.
The elections to the European Parliament bring about a change of faces but because of
its limited power the general public's interest in the institution is low. The editor
examines the first ten years of the elected Parliament, and then goes on to deal with
the elections in the member states. It should be noted that most elections were fought
on national issues, with national parties dominating the political scene.

**192 Ten European elections: campaigns and results of the 1979/81 first direct
elections to the European Parliament.**
Edited by Karlheinz Reif. London: Gower, 1985. 232p.
For each national political system European elections inevitably constitute an
additional chance to assess the nationally ruling party's electoral strength. Depending
on the state of national political strengths at the particular moment, European
elections may have considerable significance for the course of domestic politics. In this
book national specialists analyse the campaigns and results of the first direct European
Community elections in the Nine member countries in 1979 and of Greece in 1981, in
the context of national and European politics, and then proceed to assess its
consequences and subsequent developments. The lack of an index is sad.

193 Elections to the European Parliament by direct universal suffrage.
Luxembourg: European Parliament, 1977. 158p.
This publication contains the most important documents relating to direct European
elections.

European political parties

194 Socialist parties and European integration: a comparative history.
Kevin Featherstone. Manchester, England: Manchester University
Press, 1988. 370p.
A well-researched and scholarly book which gives a brief history of the socialist parties
of the member states of the European Community.

195 **Political parties in the European Community.**
Edited by Stanley Henig. London: Allen & Unwin, for the Policy
Studies Institute, 1979. 314p.

This volume is useful because it brings together material about the political parties of
the European Community. The alternative would be a search through the many
publications where the material is found in fragmented form. Apart from facts, there is
some analysis of the approach to federalism.

196 **Western European political parties: a comprehensive guide.**
Edited by Francis Jacobs. Harlow, England: Longman, 1989. 750p.

Covering all Western European countries (both EC and non-EC), this guide presents
much specially researched material which is not available elsewhere in published form.
Organized by country and covering both national and regional parties, each section
includes: a description of the national political context, a map of electoral geography,
and full details of the most recent election results in both text and tabular form.

European Court of Justice

197 **The Court of the European Community: new dimension in international
adjudication.**
Werner Feld. The Hague: Martinus Nijhoff, 1964. 127p. bibliog.

Aiming at the 'uninitiated reader', Feld attempts to set the establishment and work of
the Court in the framework of the political integration of Europe. He also raises
questions, such as how judges should be appointed. If they are political appointments
how can they remain completely independent if their reappointment depends on
governments? He does not believe that every judge needs to have judicial experience
before appointment and he also argues for a two-tier system rather than the present
Court of a single instance.

198 **The Court of Justice of the European Coal and Steel Community.**
D. C. Valentine. The Hague: Martinus Nijhoff; London: Batsford,
1955. 273p.

This was the first monograph on the Court of Justice of the European Coal and Steel
Community. It deals with ratification debates in the parliaments of the six member
states, the organization of the Court, its competence and procedure, cases pending
before the Court, and its proposed future development.

199 **The Court of Justice of the European Communities.**
Translated and edited by D. C. Valentine with a foreword by Judge
A. M. Donner. London: Stevens; South Hackensack, New Jersey:
Rothman, 1965. 2 vols. bibliog.

Volume 1 provides explanations of the structures and procedures of the Court and
examines, article by article, the Court's jurisdiction under the Treaties of the ECSC,
the EEC and Euratom. Volume 2 contains all the decisions of the ECSC Court until

1958 when it was unified with the present Court, and gives the decisions of the unified Court until 1960.

Synopsis of the work of the Court of Justice of the European Communities. *See* item no. 599.

Diplomatic relationships

200 **Diplomatic trends in the European Community.**
Christopher Hill, William Wallace. *International Affairs*, vol. 55, no. 1 (1979), p. 47–66.
This article stemmed from a pilot study on 'The Future of European Diplomacy', commissioned by the European Cultural Foundation from Chatham House. It gives details of the emergence of Community representation, examines how this will develop, and queries whether national diplomatic services will eventually wither away.

201 **Permanent representations of the member states to the EC.**
Fiona Hays Renshaw, Christian Lesquesne, Pedro Majer Lopez. *Journal of Common Market Studies*, vol. 28, no. 2 (Dec. 1989), p. 119–39.
A rare and stimulating examination of the rôle and working of the member states' permanent representations, meeting as COREPER (Committee of Permanent Representatives, i.e., EC ambassadors in Brussels). The authors sketch the legal background to COREPER, the composition, organization and rôle of representations and their work. A particular examination is made of the differing representations of France, Ireland and Spain, and the article discusses the effect that national viewpoints have on their functions and how COREPER members play a rôle, through their mutual relationships, in building a European identity.

Regional Policy

202 **Regional problems and policies in Italy and France.**
Kevin Allen, M. C. MacLennan. London: Allen & Unwin, 1970.
352p. (University of Glasgow Social and Economic Studies, no. 9).
A study of the evolution of regional policy in Italy and France, with a useful appendix
on British regional policy and the likely impact of Britain's membership of the EEC.

203 **Regional disequilibria in Europe: backward areas in industrialized
countries. A multinational comparative research.**
European Coordination Center for Research and Documentation in
Social Sciences, Vienna, with an introduction by S. Goenman,
P. Turčan. Brussels: Editions de l'Institut de Sociologie, Université
Libre de Bruxelles, 1968. 611p. bibliog.
An account of post-war activity in regional policy. The text is in French and English.

204 **La Question régionale.** (The regional question.)
J. F. Gravier. Paris: Flammarion, 1970. 233p.
An examination of regional problems and policy in Europe, with a plea for dividing
Europe into natural regions with specialist commissions to run them.

205 **Regional policy in Britain and the Six: the problems of the development
areas.**
Harold Lind.
Community regional policy.
Christopher Flockton. London: Chatham House and PEP, 1970. 76p.
At the end of the 1960s studies on regional policy in the EEC were in short supply.
Both these studies, contained in one volume, are useful as an analysis of the situation
in 1970.

206 **Regional policy.**
Colin Mellors, Nigel Copperthwaite.   London: Routledge, 1990. 240p.
The European Community is committed to promoting 'economic and social cohesion'
across the regions. This guide explains how the European Regional Development Fund
operates and its relationship to other sources of funding from the EC.

207 **Regional impact of Community policies in Europe.**
Edited by Willem Molle, Riccardo Cappellin.   Aldershot, England:
Avebury, 1988. 199p. bibliog.
This work consists of a series of essays, mainly by economists, on the spatial and
economic effects of EC regional policy. It is extremely useful that much material,
which was fairly inaccessible, has been brought together. An important factor is the
excellent bibliography.

208 **Wales in the 1990s: a European investment region.**
Jonathan Morris, Stephen Hill.   London: Economist Intelligence Unit,
1991. 105p.
This report examines the structural transformation of the Welsh economy with its
growth in private services and light industry; the key issues facing Wales, such as the
onset of the unified market; prospects for the region, including a five-year forecast, as
well as the physical infrastructure, labour resources, grants and incentives and case-
studies of foreign investment.

209 **The European Community's regional fund.**
Ross B. Talbot.   Oxford: Pergamon, 1977. 281p.
A useful study of regional policy up to 1976. It is divided into four parts: the EEC's
search for a regional policy from the signing of the Treaty of Rome to 1972; proposals
made in 1973; the establishment of the Community's Regional Development Fund in
1974; and subsequent developments.

210 **European regional incentives.**
Edited by Douglas Yuill, Kevin Allen, John Bachtler, Fiona
Wishlade.   Sevenoaks, England: Bowker-Saur, 1990. 10th ed. 534p.
A directory and review of regional grants and other aid available for industrial and
business expansion, and also of those for relocation in the member states of the
European Community and Sweden. The first section of the book analyses major policy
trends across all thirteen countries, and includes comparative tables and maps. The
reference section gives key information for all schemes on a country-by-country basis:
incentive values, eligibility criteria, application procedures, recent changes to and
history of the award, and contact addresses.

European Regional Development Fund.
See item no. 588.

Internal Market and Customs Union

General

211 **European economic integration.**
Edited by Bela Balassa.   Amsterdam: North-Holland; New York:
American Elsevier, 1975. 416p.
Although this book is mainly about EEC integration, it also deals briefly with EFTA
affairs. It covers the 1950s, 1960s and early 1970s and suggests that the EEC is at the
crossroads, barriers have gone down but little true integration has taken place. The
obstacles, according to the writers, are political rather than economic.

212 **European union: fortress or democracy?: towards a democratic market
and a new economic order.**
Michael Barratt Brown.   Nottingham, England: Spokesman for
European Labour Forum, 1991. 128p.
The author, an international economist, examines some of the problems involved in
preventing the emergence of a fortress mentality in Europe as a response to the
catastrophic situation outside. He raises fundamental questions about the failure of
economic command systems in the east to deliver the goods, the equal failure of the
capitalist world market to meet the needs of more than a small minority of the world's
people, and the disastrous results for all from rising debts and falling incomes in the
consequent recourse to internecine struggle and military adventure. In doing so, he
offers some suggestions for new forms of economic development, new ways of making
the market democratic, and new types of trade relations which are both fairer and
more environmentally sustainable.

213 **European border controls: who needs them?**
Alan Butt Philip. London: Royal Institute of International Affairs,
1989. 36p. (Discussion Paper 19).

The Single European Act commits the member states of the European Community to
establish by 31 December 1992 an internal market comprising an 'area without internal
frontiers', in which persons as well as goods, services and capital can move freely. In
1985, the Benelux, French and German governments signed the intergovernmental
Schengen Agreement, committing themselves to a gradual dismantling of border
controls between their five countries. These objectives touch on many important and
sensitive issues regarding the movement of people, as well as goods. This paper aims to
sketch the essentials of what has been agreed by mid-1989, to highlight the key issues,
and to stimulate further debate.

214 **Barriers to takeovers in the European Community.**
Coopers & Lybrand, for the Department of Trade and Industry.
London: HMSO, 1989. 3 vols.

A very detailed study of cross-border takeovers in Europe. It implies that takeovers of
British firms by foreign companies are easier than the other way round, but this is not
necessarily so.

215 **The European Common Market: an analysis of commercial policy.**
Isaiah Frank. London: Stevens, for the London Institute of World
Affairs, 1961. 324p. bibliog.

This book is about the commercial, economic and monetary effects of the Treaty of
Rome. The author has aimed at analysing rather than describing. There are six
sections, each of which is well documented: commercial policy in regional co-operation
before the Rome treaty; the treatment of trade restrictions in the Rome treaty;
economic integration and traditional commercial policy; global aspects of Common
Market tariff policy; tariff problems posed by the European Free Trade Association
(EFTA); and quota problems of the Common Market.

216 **The political economy of European integration.**
Edited by Paolo Guerrieri, Pier Carlo Padoan. Hemel Hempstead,
England: Harvester Wheatsheaf, 1989. 320p.

The volume brings together leading contributors from North America and Europe to
examine a number of key aspects of the economic integration process in Europe. It
focuses on macroeconomic policy co-ordination and financial integration, and analyses
the record of the European Monetary System. It makes a major contribution to our
understanding of these issues and will be of interest to economists, those studying
international political economy, and policy-makers.

217 **The political economy of European trade: an introduction to the trade
policies of the EEC.**
R. C. Hine. Brighton, England: Wheatsheaf; New York: St Martin's
Press, 1985. 294p.

This comprehensive study of the European Community trade policies to 1984 examines
both the internal and the external advantages. The greatest external advantages have
been with the USA. The EC and the US have similar economies and hence General

49

Internal Market and Customs Union. The Single European Act (1992)

Agreement on Tariffs and Trade (GATT) tariff reductions led to intra-trade creation. Success with Japan was more difficult because Europeans have failed to penetrate Japanese markets.

218　**Merger and competition policy in the European Community.**
Alexis Jacquemin (et al.), edited by P. H. Admiraal.　Oxford: Blackwell, 1991. 156p.

Four leading industrial economists examine this central issue, showing that there is a tendency to overrate the benefits of mergers and underestimate their costs.

219　**Patterns and prospects of Common Market trade.**
George M. Taber, preface by Roger Beardwood.　London: Peter Owen, 1974. 192p.

A popular concise study of trade patterns of the EEC for the first half of 1973 contrasted with the structure of trade for EEC countries in earlier periods. One major point made is that Taber found no evidence that the British government attempted to study the idea of developing the Commonwealth as an economic community.

220　**The competition rules of the European Community. An essential guide to articles 85 and 86 of the EEC treaty.**
Oxford: Manches, 1990. 28p.

A guide for businessmen to the competition rules of the EC, consisting of a short introduction, an explanation of the scope of the rules, the consequences of breaching them, ways in which infringement can be avoided, an investigation of articles 85 and 86, and the way in which they affect various types of agreement, clauses in agreements, and monopoly practices. The booklet is intended as a general summary of the law as of October 1990. Although less up to date, *Competition policy: European and international trends and practices* by A. E. Walsh and John Paxton (London: Macmillan, 1975. 196p.) is a useful analysis of Articles 85 and 86 of the Treaty of Rome which were framed to ensure that non-tariff restrictions caused by restrictive practices should not distort the basic aims of the Common Market. There is a listing of decisions by the Commission and the Court of Justice, to 1974, and also comparative studies of competition policy in the major countries of the world.

The Single European Act (1992)

221　**The 1992 challenge from Europe: development of the European Community's internal market.**
Michael Calingaert.　Washington, DC: National Planning Association, 1988. 164p.

The author has written a full-scale review of the EC's efforts to bring about a fully integrated market. With completion of the ambitious EC economic integration programme scheduled for 1992, this interim assessment outlines the background and prospective scope of the programme and covers the significance of areas being addressed, the changing institutional framework, the political pressures at work, and the structural changes that the market is expected to undergo by 1992. The author gives special attention to anticipated developments that will be of major importance to US firms which have trade, investment and other commercial ties with the twelve EC nations. He also discusses the implications of these developments for US public policies and government actions.

222 **The European challenge 1992: the benefits of a single market.**
Edited by Paulo Cecchini. Aldershot, England: Gower, 1988. 180p.

The core findings of this book are that EC governments will give business the chance of seizing the opportunities on offer if they implement in full and on schedule the European Commission's 1992 programme for eliminating the barriers still segmenting European markets into 12 national components. The overall cost of these barriers is estimated at 5 per cent of Community gross domestic product (GDP), and the benefit of their removal, if accompanied by supportive economic policies, could be as high as 7 per cent of GDP in the medium term. This is a summary edition of the 16-volume report into the 'Cost of non-Europe', known as the Cecchini Report (see item no. 251).

223 **Europe relaunched: truths and illusions on the way to 1992.**
Nicholas Colchester, David Buchan. London: Hutchinson/Economist Books, 1990. 256p.

Europe relaunched explores the reaction of governments both inside and outside the European Community to the challenge of the single market, the development of the relationship between the new democracies of Eastern Europe and the Community, and the kind of market those in business will find themselves operating. It also contains two appendices: Lord Cockfield's blueprint for the single market, and the other giving details of commissioners and their portfolios.

224 **1992 – The struggle for Europe: a critical evaluation of the European Community.**
Tony Cutler, Colin Haslam, John Williams, Karel Williams. Oxford: Berg, 1989. 192p. bibliog.

All the economic research into 1992 was commissioned and paid for by the European Commission which, naturally, makes strong claims for the economic benefits likely to flow from the Single Market. There is, therefore, scope for an independent critical evaluation of the costs and benefits of 1992. The political right lauds 1992 as a further triumph for free markets and the left as a means of getting otherwise unobtainable progressive social policies. Yet, closer scrutiny raises serious doubts about the validity of the claims and hopes on both sides. The authors, with a left-wing bias, examine the European Commission's micro-economic model of Europe on which the claims are based, and highlight a series of questionable and implausible assumptions, particularly on the likely economies of scale and the so-called positive effects of competition and merger. They also raise the question of British manufacturing, already suffering from a massive redistribution of output and employment to mainland Europe, which, in their opinion, can only suffer further loss after 1992.

Internal Market and Customs Union. The Single European Act (1992)

225 **Whose Europe? Competing visions for 1992.**
Ralf Dahrendorf, John Hoskyns, Victoria Curzon Price, Ben Roberts,
Geoffrey E. Wood, Evan Davis, L. S. Sealy, foreword by Cento
Veljanovski. London: Institute of Economic Affairs, 1989. 106p.

This publication brings together a group of scholars and contributors to consider
whether the EC has become a corporatist and over-centralized political Leviathan
controlled by an unaccountable bureaucracy in Brussels, or whether the harmonization
directives and proposals for a European Monetary Union, a common currency, a
European Central Bank and a Social Charter are prerequisites for the single market.
They examine the trends, details, failures and consequences of the 1992 Single Market
programme.

226 **Europe without frontiers – completing the internal market.**
Foreword by Jacques Delors, preface by Martin Bangemann.
Luxembourg: Office of Official Publications of the Community, 1989.
68p. bibliog. (European documentation 2/1989).

This official publication sets out to explain the main aspects of the Community's
programme and state what progress had been made by 1989. It has a particularly good
list of over 100 pamphlets and articles, both official and unofficial, for further reading
on the Single Market.

227 **Your business in 1992.**
James Dewhurst. London: Rosters, 1989. 304p.

Dewhurst analyses the workings of the European market, examines the implications
for decision-makers, and outlines strategies for coping with the new business
environment.

228 **1992 strategies for the single market.**
James W. Dudley. London: Kogan Page, in association with the
Chartered Institute of Management Accountants, 1989. 400p.

A practical guide for businessmen to exploit the opportunities in the biggest-spending
market. It does not treat 1992 as an option, but as a challenge. As the single market
will touch every business in terms of legal issues, threats and opportunities this is a
useful guide. Chapter 16 'Making it happen' offers a superb checklist.

229 **The economics of 1992: the EC Commission's assessment of the
economic effects of completing the internal market.**
Michael Emerson. Oxford: Oxford University Press, 1988. 304p.

The European Commission felt the need to establish that the removal of trade and
other barriers by 1992 would definitely bring economic advantages. This study is by
members of the Commission's Directorate-General for Economic and Financial Affairs
and contains an account of the conclusions of the study. It is suggested that the
potential gains could be an increase in the Community's gross domestic product (GDP)
of up to 6.5 per cent.

230 **European internal market policy.**
Kevin Featherstone. London: Routledge, 1989. 176p.

This publication offers comprehensive and up-to-date information about '1992', presented in a clear and readily accessible format. In an extensive introduction, it explains how policy programmes emerged and discusses the implications for the future.

231 **1992, who's ready?**
Kevin Featherstone, Kenneth Dyson. Bradford, England: Horton, for the Department of European Studies, University of Bradford, 1990. 86p.
Just how prepared are firms to meet the challenge of the Single European Market after 1992? What action are companies taking to prepare themselves? What help and support might public bodies offer them? These questions are asked in this research report based on a study involving a survey of over 900 firms. The findings of the survey suggest serious cause for concern that companies may be misjudging and underestimating the impact of a single European market on their operations and may be inadequately prepared as a result.

232 **Doing business in the European Community.**
Paul Gibbs. London: Kogan Page, 1990. 240p.
The first part of this book sets the scene by providing the necessary background information on what is actually going to happen in 1992, what marketing opportunities open up, what strategies are needed for coping with 1992, and what finance, grants and loans are available from the EC. The second part is a detailed guide to the cultural, social and economic differences that exist in each of the member countries.

233 **Towards 1992: Europe at the crossroads.**
Edited by Paul Hainsworth. Newtownabbey, Northern Ireland: University of Ulster, 1990. 91p.
This collection of short essays, seen from a Northern Ireland viewpoint, deals with some of the most salient aspects of the path towards a Single European Market, the 1992 process and the emerging Europe of the 1990s. Amongst the themes dealt with are British traditions and European integration, Mrs Thatcher's Europe, regional and economic aspects of 1992, women and 1992, the enlargement of the Community, the Commission and 1992, European law, and political party perspectives and 1992 (in Northern Ireland). A distinct sub-theme of the collection is Northern Ireland and the current phase of European integration. However, other chapters turn more to the broader aspects and the essays should appeal to the general reader.

234 **The single European market.**
James Hogan. London: Macmillan, 1990. 600p.
An excellent guide for businessmen. It assembles many business information sources in one volume, offering an introduction to key areas of the single market activity and guidance on European Community legislation.

235 **The European internal market: trade and competition.**
Edited by Alexis Jacquemin, André Sapir. Oxford: Oxford University Press, 1989. 382p.
The editors have brought together articles on European integration published since 1960. It is divided into three parts: the first deals with the theory of customs unions, the second with the effects of integration, and the third part discusses policy related to 1992 and the Single European Act.

Internal Market and Customs Union. The Single European Act (1992)

236 **Towards 1992: state aids to industry.**

F. Knox.   London: Trade and Tariffs Research, 1989. 81p.

This publication compares GATT and EC principles on subsidies. EC principles are laid down in the Treaty of Rome, under Articles 92 to 94, and subsidy cases in the European Court of Justice. It gives figures of subsidies by country and industry, and how these have been changing. There is also information on EC aids to industry.

237 **The European Community and the challenge of the future.**

Edited by Juliet Lodge.   London: Pinter, 1989. 300p.

Describes the workings of the European Community with an eye on the changes to be marked by 1992. The second half examines EC relations with the rest of the world.

238 **The European challenge: industry's response to the 1992 programme.**

Edited by David Mayes, foreword by Michael Emerson.   Hemel Hempstead, England: Harvester Wheatsheaf, 1991. 320p.

Provides an assessment and detailed analysis of the impact of the 1992 programme to complete the single market in the European Community. The Cecchini Report originally estimated that the impact could increase national income by as much as 4.5 to 7 per cent. This book raises serious questions about the magnitude of the benefits of the programme. It was commissioned by the European Commission and contains studies for eleven separate industries: aerospace; airlines; chemicals, pharmaceuticals and man-made fibres; electronic components and consumer electronics; iron and steel; machine tools; motor cars; office machinery and information technology; railways and railway equipment; trucks. Each study describes the structure of the industry and assesses the single market measures which affect it, before going on to consider the changes which are under way and the internal and external strategies adopted by each industry in response to the 1992 initiative.

239 **European competition policy.**

Edited by Peter Montagnon.   London: Pinter, 1990. 135p.

(A Chatham House Paper).

This study is by the West European Programme of the Royal Institute of International Affairs. It argues that the full benefits of the single market will not be attained without an effective competition policy. The European Community is now set on a course which will produce a genuine European competition policy in place of the present set of varied and uncertain national ones.

240 **The economics of 1992.**

Edited by Henry Neuburger.   London: European Parliamentary Labour Party, 1989. 65p.

This report, commissioned by the British Labour group of members of the European Parliament, analyses the action which must be taken to attain a socialist way forward for the EC.

54

Internal Market and Customs Union. The Single European Act (1992)

241   **1992 and beyond.**
John Palmer.   London: Her Majesty's Stationery Office, 1990. 92p.
The European editor of the *Guardian* looks at new questions on the European agenda including enlargement of the Community, relations with Eastern Europe, the calls for democratic control of Community decision-making, and the creation of a 'citizen's Europe' of social and political rights.

242   **Europe's domestic market.**
Jacques Pelkmans, L. Alan Winters.   London: Routledge, for the Royal Institute of International Affairs, 1988. 150p.
This Chatham House Paper is a successful attempt to study the background, the micro- and macro-economic implications, and the likely outcome of the creation of a single internal market in the European Community by 1992.

243   **Chambers of Commerce: the challenge of the 1992 EEC internal market.**
A. M. W. Platt.   London: London Chamber of Commerce, 1989. 36p.
Compares five European chambers of commerce operating under a public law status system (Amsterdam, Hamburg, Munich, Madrid and Paris) with the London Chamber of Commerce. It describes the status, structure and services of these chambers, and shows how services to business provided by those five European chambers benefit from the public law status system under which they operate.

244   **1992: Europe's last chance? From Common Market to Single Market.**
Victoria Curzon Price.   London: Institute of Economic Affairs, 1988. 46p. (Nineteenth Wincott Memorial Lecture, Occasional Paper 81).
The author believes that the Single Market based on the EC White Paper and the Single European Act is a fantastic dream, a pure exercise in deregulation. It says: give a maximum of say to markets, a minimum to Brussels and get national governments off our backs. The gains from the Single Market are potentially considerable. There is no reason why the average European should not be as well off as the average American, and this gives us scope in Europe to increase our incomes on average by 50 per cent. But there is no gain without pain. The restructuring process has hardly started; it is a matter of closing down some plants and opening others, concentrating production where it is most efficient, capturing economies of scale. This process is bound to create social and political tensions, and the author asks whether people are prepared to let the market perform its job of sorting out the European economy on the basis of free competition, with a minimum of social policy to blunt the process. She sums up by saying: 'The Single Market involves a transfer of sovereignty to market forces, not to Brussels; allows national differences to flourish, not to perish; decentralises rather than concentrates economic power.'

245   **Delors versus 1992?**
B. C. Roberts.   London: Bruges Group, 1989. 10p. (Occasional Paper 1).
In this sharp and controversial pamphlet Roberts puts forward the substance of the anti-interventionist case against the Social Charter, then at the discussion stage. He argues that the Charter will 'threaten the economic benefits promised by 1992, and that 'not only would it lead to a dangerous degree of political centralisation, but it would

disturb indigenous employment relations systems . . . and would obstruct their adaptation to the needs of employers and workers'.

246 **Developments in European retailing.**
Edited by Nitin Sanghavi, Alan Treadgold. Yeovil, England: Dower House, 1990. 128p.

The book is essential reading for all those in or associated with the retail sector. It is in two parts: the first focuses specifically on European development in three sectors, food, department stores, and clothing and footwear; the second highlights crucial issues of change across the whole retail sector, notably the development opportunities for retailers in continental Europe and the cost of exploiting those opportunities, cross-border alliances, foreign entrants into UK retailing, and the way UK retailers can and do respond to the single market in 1992. In spite of the recent strong emergence of cross-border alliances between European retail groups, and the fact that nearly all the sector leaders in the UK have moved in recent years to develop a strong trading presence overseas, a limited number of sectors in the UK look relatively underdeveloped in contrast to continental Europe. The editors conclude that a number of features in the UK retail environment, notably the open environment for acquisitions, low barriers to business development, high levels of profitability, good information services and market size considerations, make the UK attractive for foreign retailers who are planning for the longer term.

247 **The smaller company and '1992'.**
David Stoker, Vincent Benson. Yeovil, England: Dower House, 1990. 63p.

The European Community holds the view that small firms, with their growth potential, their flexibility to cope with change, and their ability to innovate, should be encouraged and supported. To this end the Commission has promoted the SME (small and medium-sized enterprise) task force to a full directorate-general (DG23). It is therefore ironical that, at the very time that the worth and value of small firms is at last being recognized, an economic environment is being created which presents greater threats to SMEs than to larger companies. The challenges of the single market for the SME are not those of a multinational writ smaller, i.e., the differences are not simply those of scale, but are inherently different. The book is intended both for SME owner/managers and, in particular, for those who assist and advise small companies.

248 **The single European market: prospects for economic integration.**
Roger Vickermann. Hemel Hempstead, England: Philip Allan, 1991. 224p.

Much has been written about the failure of the European Community to achieve any real integration of the European economies and despite the great hopes of the 1992 programme there is much criticism of the claims made about the potential economic benefits. The author sets out to reassess the basis of the single market in the context of economic integration as a process. He focuses on the way that the decisions of individual consumers and producers will be affected by this process and hence provides a dynamic analysis. A particular theme of the book is the changing regional dimension of the Community and the critical rôle of the infrastructure in the integration process. A series of sector case-studies (hi-tech industries; textiles and clothing; food, drink and tobacco; motor vehicles; financial services; and tourism) is used to illustrate the process. The book is designed to provide a unified introduction to the key economic issues raised by the European Community and the completion of the single market, and to complement more orthodox texts on the European Community. But the consumer should be king and *Banker's racket or consumer benefit?: a consumer view of the single European Market for financial services* by Jeremy Mitchell (London: Policy Studies Institute, 1991. 192p.) looks at all aspects of the financial services. Mitchell explains that the European Community's plans for a single market for banking, insurance and other financial services involve continuing public and private debate about what the effects will be on banks and other financial institutions, but that much less attention has been paid to the consequences for individual consumers. Yet if consumers do not gain from the changes that are taking place, the single market cannot be counted as a success. This book examines how the single market will affect consumers' use of banking services, consumer credit, mortgages, payment cards, insurance, unit trusts and investment services. The author weighs in the balance the possible benefits of greater competition and the threats to consumer protection and the privacy of personal data.

249 **Vision versus vision.**
Gerard Wissels. *The European*, vol. 1, no. 3 (May–June 1987), p. 17.
This article attacks the internal market proposals and studies the opposing visions for the EC, i.e., the 'Community approach' versus 'market orientation'.

250 **1992: myths and realities.**
London: London Business School, Centre for Business Strategy, 1989. 123p. (Report Series).
Looks beyond the discussion of 1992, and assesses the realities of what the programme means for business opportunities and business behaviour. In five different essays, the report looks at: the effect of an open European market on trade; the choice between diversity and scale; the business implications of fiscal harmonization; the impact of the Channel tunnel on 1992; and the integration of European financial services.

251 **Research on the 'Cost of non-Europe': basic findings (The Cecchini Report).**
Luxembourg: Office for Official Publications of the European Communities, 1988. 16 vols.
The official *Cecchini Report*, launched in 1986, into the present cost of market fragmentation points out the benefits of the creation of a Single Market. It consists of:
Vol. 1 Basic studies: executive summaries, 1988. 576p. Contains the executive summaries of the basic reports.
Vol. 2 Studies on the economy of integration, 1988. 652p. Analyses the savings from economies of scale and market structure, including micro- and macro-economic effects.
Vol. 3 The completion of the internal market: a summary of European industry's perception of the likely effects.
Gernot Nerb, 1988. 309p.
Vol. 4 The 'Cost of non-Europe': border-related controls and administrative formalities: an illustration in the road haulage sector.
Ernst & Whinney, 1988. 280p.
Vol. 5 The 'Cost of non-Europe': in public-sector procurement, 1988. vol. A, 552p., Vol. B, 278p.
Vol. 6 Technical barriers in the EC: some case studies on the 'Cost of non-Europe', 1988. 242p.

Internal Market and Customs Union. The Single European Act (1992)

Vol. 7 The 'Cost of non-Europe': obstacles to transborder business activity.
Wolfgang Hager and Heimfried Wolf, 1988. 154p.
Vol. 8 The 'Cost of non-Europe' for business services.
Peat Marwick McLintock, 1988. 140p.
Vol. 9 The 'Cost of non-Europe' in financial services.
Price Waterhouse, 1988. 494p.
Vol. 10 The benefits of completing the internal market for telecommunication equipment, services in the Community.
Jurgen Muller, 1988. 197p.
Vol. 11 The EC 92 automobile sector.
Ludvigsen Associates Ltd, 1988. 350p.
Vol. 12 The 'Cost of non-Europe' in the foodstuffs industry.
Group MAC, 1988. Vol. A, 424p., Vol. B, 328p.
Vol. 13 The 'Cost of non-Europe' in the construction industry (Le 'coût de la non-Europe' des produits de construction).
BIPE, 1988. 168p. (Available in French only).
Vol. 14 The 'Cost of non-Europe' in the textile clothing industry.
Michael Breitenacher, Sergio Paba and Gianpaolo Rossini, 1988. 256p.
Vol. 15 The pharmaceutical industry.
Economics Advisory Group Ltd, 1988. 182p.
Vol. 16 The internal markets of North America: fragmentation and integration in the USA and Canada.
Jacques Pelkmans and Marc Vanheukelen, 1988. 176p.

Political Union

General

252 **Europe's futures, Europe's choices: models of western Europe in the 1970s.**
Edited by Alastair Buchan.   London: Chatto & Windus, for the Institute of Strategic Studies, 1969. 167p.

A group study by members of the Institute but the whole written by Alastair Buchan, the then director. A series of models of future co-operation between European countries are examined. Each model is analysed for its internal and external consequences and particularly the impact each would have on USA, USSR and Eastern Europe. No model was ideal but it was felt that with compromise a solution to European co-operation was possible. Buchan quotes 'The time for Grand Schemes is over; we are moving out of our architectural period in Europe into the age of manoeuvre'.

253 **Europe's future: the grand alternatives.**
David P. Calleo, preface by Donald Tyerman.   London: Hodder and Stoughton, 1967. 192p.

Professor Calleo believes that a federal Europe is impossible and argues for an Atlantic association supported by a group of European states with the leadership coming from Britain. Britain could, he argues, sever its special relationship with the US and form a tight Anglo-French alliance. Although published in 1967, there are some stimulating ideas here which are still very readable all these years later and at a time when Europe is in a state of flux from the Atlantic to the Urals.

254 **Politics and bureaucracy in the European Community: a portrait of the Commission of the E.E.C.**
David Coombes.   London: PEP and Allen & Unwin, 1970. 343p.

An analysis of the central issue of European integration, namely, whether the institutions, established by the Treaty of Rome, can bring about the envisaged economic and political union. Coombes believes that they cannot and thinks that the Commission is too preoccupied with mediation with governments, a situation which has in turn led to greater bureaucracy. Coombes is not sure of the remedies but suggests that what is required is some 'electoral process on party lines designed to bring power to a European government with a distinct programme of action at the federal level'.

255 **The European Community: a superpower in the making.**
Johan Galtung.   Oslo: Universitetforlaget; London: Allen & Unwin, 1973. 195p. (PRIO Studies from the International Peace Research Institute, Oslo; PRIO Publication, no. 22–21).

Galtung argues that in the long term 'the Community is an effort to turn history backwards, only adding a dimension of modern technology' and that it would create a Europe with its centre in the West which would be to the disadvantage of the world proletariat and the world community in general. These arguments had some impact in the 'no' referendum in Norway.

256 **Europe in the making.**
Johan Galtung.   New York: Crane Rusak, 1989. 190p.

In his book *The European Community: a superpower in the making* (q.v.), the author gave his views on the EC. In this new study he continues the theme and argues for a Europe of twenty-nine states rather than an inward-looking twelve.

257 **The European idea.**
Lord Gladwyn.   London: Weidenfeld & Nicolson, 1966. 159p.

In the first chapters of this work there is a recapitulation of the European political position following the 1963 breakdown of UK entry into the EEC. Lord Gladwyn advocates a United States of Europe and this is a step forward in new and improved reasoning.

258 **An idea of Europe.**
Richard Hoggart, Douglas Johnson.   London: Chatto & Windus, 1987. 154p.

Charlemagne, Napoleon and Hitler used armed force to try to unite Europe. The EC is young and it is difficult to say what the outcome of plans for unification will be, especially now that East Europe comes into any future equation. This is a stimulating book which explores all sorts of avenues but is, perhaps understandably, short on predictions.

259 **The healing of Europe.**
Christopher Layton.   London: Federal Trust for Education and
Research, 1990. 36p.

This essay explores the new horizons opened up by the liberation of Eastern Europe
and by German unity. The author argues that the Community method, which has
reconciled West Germany with its western neighbours, must be extended, in the 1990s,
to Europe as a whole.

260 **European union: the European Community in search of a future.**
Edited by Juliet Lodge, foreword by Altiero Spinelli.   London:
Macmillan, 1986. 239p.

This publication deals with the European Parliament's draft treaty on European union.
It shows how the predominantly moderate MEPs of the first directly elected European
Parliament were led to adopt a quasi-constituent role. Their analysis of party and
national attitudes demonstrates how a consensus was created in setting up the
institutional committee even though no single established group could take the
initiative. Other chapters, taken together, give the reader a strong sense of the
coherence of the Parliament's bid to win immediate power for itself, the Commission,
and the Court. *Draft treaty on European union: synopsis of section on European
political union* by David Millar (Edinburgh: Europa Institute of Edinburgh University,
1991. 23p.) is a synopsis of, with some commentaries on, the new Articles that
emerged at the European Council's meeting at Maastricht in December 1991.

261 **The idea of Europe: problems of national and transnational identity.**
Edited by Brian Nelson, David Roberts, Walter Veit.   Oxford: Berg,
1991. 192p.

An examination of the historical dimension of the European idea and the problems
facing European integration in the 1990s.

262 **West European politics since 1945: the shaping of the European
Community.**
Roger Morgan.   London: Batsford, 1972. 243p.

Morgan deals with the recovery of Europe following the devastation of the Second
World War and pinpoints both the progress and the lack of progress in achieving a
federal Europe.

263 **The logic of unity: a geography of the European Economic Community.**
Geoffrey Parker.   London; New York: Longman, 1981. 3rd ed. 208p.

An interesting and refreshing study which transcends national boundaries and gives the
geo-economic case for European integration. Obviously many factors work against the
logic of unity; these include nationalism, long-established methods of conducting
economic activity and traditional thinking, but the author presses on to his last chapter
which examines the concept of a European Federation by the year 2000.

264 **Landmarks in European unity: twenty-two texts on European integration.**
Edited by S. Patijn. Leyden, The Netherlands: Sijthoff, 1970. 223p.
This handy volume of source material in both English and French would be useful to students. Twenty-two documents are included, beginning in 1946 with Churchill's Zürich University speech and ending with the Hague Summit of 1969.

265 **The dynamics of European union.**
Edited by Roy Pryce. London: Routledge, 1987. 320p.
A survey of the efforts made over the last forty years to achieve European union. It explains succinctly the 'ebbs and flows' of enthusiasms for union.

266 **Europe at risk.**
Alan Watson. London: Harrap, 1972. 224p.
Watson feels that Western Europe is at risk from the 'American challenge' to national economies, a resurgent Germany, and the failure of national political systems to guide the destiny of their countries. He advocates tighter unification of Europe.

Federalism

267 **Federalism and European union: political ideas, influences and strategies in the European Community, 1972–1987.**
Michael Burgess. London: Routledge, 1989. 225p.
This book examines the various types of federalism and comes out in favour of the Brussels solution, but even those who are not for a closer political union will find much of interest.

268 **Mrs Thatcher, federalism and the future of Europe.**
Michael Burgess. *European Access*, 1989, 1 (February), p. 9–10.
A short angry article pointing out why Mrs Thatcher was wrong in her September 1988 speech at the College of Europe in Bruges. That was the speech in which she gave her views on the suppressing of nationhood in a federal Europe.

269 **Federal solutions to European issues.**
Edited by Bernard Burrows, Geoffrey Denton, Geoffrey Edwards.
London: Macmillan, for the Federal Trust, 1978. 225p.
The first part of this book deals with political needs and institutions and among other subjects explains why Britain needs a federal constitution and the functional aspect of federalism. There are also chapters on community institutions and community law. The second part studies some specific policy areas: monetary unification, the Community budget, industrial policy, company organization, social policy, and agriculture. The final part deals with the enlargement of the Community, foreign policy, defence, and raw material supplies. John Pinder writes on 'A Federal Community in an Ungoverned World Economy'.

270 **Federal systems of the world.**
Edited by Daniel J. Elazar.   Harlow, England: Longman, 1991. 300p.
Not strictly a European Community book, but as the debate on political union for the
Twelve gathers momentum this complete guide to federalism is a useful reference. The
details given for each federal state include: history; demography; political, economic
and judicial structure; domestic power and functions; international relations; and
culture.

271 **Britain in Federal Europe.**
John Lambert.   London: Chatto and Windus, 1968. 208p.
Lambert believes passionately in a Federal Europe and, writing in an engaging style,
he explains the differences between the Monnet and the de Gaulle approaches to
Europe.

272 **Federal Union: the pioneers. A history of federal union.**
Richard Mayne, John Pinder, John C. de V. Roberts.   London:
Macmillan, 1990. 288p.
Federalism is often depicted in Britain as an alien concept with which the British
cannot come to terms. Between 1938 and 1940, the British were the leaders in
promoting the federal idea. The organization known as Federal Union rapidly gained
both élite and mass support. Following the rejection of Churchill's offer of union to
France, it was the course of the war that diverted the British from the idea of a federal
Europe, which was at the same time taking root in the resistance movements on the
continent. This book shows how Federal Union achieved its originality and strength;
how its literature inspired a small group in the Italian Resistance who became founders
of the European federal movement; how this movement influenced the building of the
present European Community; how a small group of British federalists carried
membership of the Community – while others worked to strengthen Atlantic and world
institutions; how the British federalists contributed to thinking about the Community's
further development; and how their work has continued in the 1980s, in the context of
the Single European Act and the prospect that it will be followed by European union
in the 1990s.

273 **Federalism and international relations: the role of subnational units.**
Edited by Hans J. Michelmann, Panayotis Soldatos.   Oxford:
Clarendon Press, 1990. 322p.
The external relations of federated states will undergo much intensive study in the
1990s as the authority from the centre is weakened; this is a useful book to read during
the EC debates on political union.

274 **The political future of the European Community.**
Roy Pryce.   London: John Marshbank with the Federal Trust, 1962.
108p.
This book gives early warnings that the Community could become an irresponsible
bureaucracy, and Pryce advocates a quasi-federal union. He poses far more questions
than he answers, but it is a thoughtful and challenging work.

Political Union. Federalism

275 **After 1992: the United States of Europe.**
Ernest Wistrich, foreword by Lord Jenkins. London: Routledge,
1989. 176p.

Wistrich challenges unfettered national sovereignty and argues that the changes of 1992
will precipitate the transformation of the European Community into a full political and
economic union, organized according to federal principles. This publication examines
the monetary, economic, social and cultural dimensions of the process.

The Community and the Third World

General

276 **Does aid work?**
Robert Cassen.   Oxford: Clarendon Press, 1986. 381p.
A detailed and scholarly treatment of an emotive subject, ranging beyond the purely
European Community context (although the EC is a major concern). Cassen and his
colleagues conclude that although much aid does not work, in general aid can be said
to succeed on its own terms. The major failings detected by the authors stem from the
failure of both parties to learn from previous experience.

277 **The external economies of the EEC.**
Peter Coffey.   London: Macmillan, 1976. 118p.
The aim of this study is to present a global picture of the Community's external
economic relations from a European viewpoint. It was written in 1975, an important
year in creating a new world monetary order. There is a useful appendix listing EEC
agreements with Third World countries in April 1974.

278 **Europe: 1992 and the developing world.**
Michael Davenport, Sheila Page.   London: Overseas Development
Institute, 1991.
In this study the authors analyse the implications for developing countries of the Single
European Market. Many manufactured imports from outside the European Community will be displaced by EC production which will become more competitive. On
the other hand, the increment in Community income will raise imports of those goods
which the EC does not produce and the elimination of bilateral trading arrangements
between member states and certain less developed countries will have some significant
effects. As well as looking at the impact of 1992 on the Third World as a whole, the
study examines the interests of a number of developing countries in some detail. To a
large extent the effects of 1992 on the developing countries will turn on factors of a
more qualitative character. How will the developing countries cope with the plethora

of new Community standards? To what extent will the Community resort to trade protection – the 'Fortress Europe'? Will direct foreign investment be diverted from the less developed countries to the Community? Will 1992 lead to important changes in the international trading system? This book looks at these issues and the dangers and opportunities they pose for developing countries.

279   **Britain in Europe: impact on the Third World.**
      Haruko Fukuda.   London: Macmillan, 1973. 194p.
Fukuda looks into the future at the trading world that will exist in an enlarged Community. Her worries are that the principle expounded by GATT's most-favoured-nation clause will be eroded as more and more trading agreements are signed with the Community. She writes: 'in the long-term it is questionable whether such heavy economic and political dependence on a single market is beneficial or even desirable in terms of progress of these nations themselves'.

280   **The Common Agricultural Policy and the Less Developed Countries.**
      Alan Matthews.   London: Gill & Macmillan, 1985. 268p.
An academic and often technical survey of the links between what is still the major area of European Community activity and the Third World. The author considers the main arguments for and against food subsidies. EC intervention has tended to lower world market prices, thus reducing already low incomes.

281   **European trade policies and the developing world.**
      Edited by L. B. Mennes, Jacob Kol.   London: Croom Helm, 1988.
      368p.
A collection of academic essays which examines particular aspects of the European Community's trade with the Third World, and which places EC trade in its world context.

282   **Africa and the Common Market.**
      P. N. C. Okigbo.   London: Longmans, 1967. 183p.
An important study for anyone wishing to understand the main trends and alignments of African trade in the 1960s and 1970s.

283   **The EEC and the Third World: a survey.**
      Edited by Christopher Stevens.   London: Hodder & Stoughton,
      1981–87.
A series of annual volumes providing a forum for academic and political consideration of specific topics in European Community–Third World relations. The individual volumes provide important background material to an understanding of the rôle of the EC in the moral and economic debate on the Third World. The six volumes (available separately) are: 1981, *A general collection of essays* (150p.); 1982, *Hunger in the world* (177p.); 1983, *The Atlantic rift* (242p.); 1984, *Re-negotiating Lomé* (the Second and Third Lomé Conventions) (198p.); 1985, *Pressure group policies and development* (180p.); 1986 (no volume issued); 1987, *Europe and the international division of labour* (173p.).

284 **European Communities' single market: the challenge of 1992 for sub-Saharan Africa.**
Alfred Tovias.   Washington, DC: World Bank, 1990. 78p.
This pamphlet, a World Bank discussion paper (no. 100), pinpoints the difficulties and challenges for sub-Saharan African countries engaged in trade with the European Communities.

285 **Costs of protectionism to developing countries: an analysis for selected agricultural products.**
Joachim Zietz, Alberto Valdés.   Washington, DC: World Bank, 1986. 98p.
This is one of the World Bank's Working Papers (no. 769). It is an analysis of the impact of the European Communities policies on selected agricultural products.

286 **Britain, the EEC and the Third World.**
London: Overseas Development Institute, 1971. 91p.
Report of an international conference, jointly sponsored by the Society for International Development and the Overseas Development Institute, and held at the Royal Society in April 1971.

287 **Europe 1992 and the developing countries.**
Journal of Common Market Studies, vol. 29, no. 2 (Dec. 1990). 142p.
A special issue devoted to the implications of the Single Market for the Community's relations with developing countries. Individual essays deal with trade in primary products and manufactures, the overall position of the 'New Europe' *vis-à-vis* its Third World trading partners, and with the impact of '1992' on the Maghreb and sub-Saharan Africa. A cautious, even concerned, tone is set by the concluding essay which warns that, after all, the Single European Market is a device designed and initiated by Europeans for Europeans, through a legislative system into which less developed countries (LDCs) have no direct input.

288 **The European Community and the developing countries: a policy for the future.**
London: Federal Trust for Education and Research, 1988. 45p.
This report of a Federal Trust Study Group (chaired by John Leech) examines present and future relations between the EC and developing nations.

289 **Exporting to industrial countries: prospects for businesses in developing countries.**
Washington, DC: World Bank, 1990. 40p.
This paper, from the International Finance Corporation economics department, analyses what strategy should be adopted by Third World countries when exporting to the European Communities.

Lomé Conventions

290 **The EC internal market, Lomé IV and the ACP countries.**
Stefan Brune. *Intereconomics*, vol. 25, no. 4 (July–Aug. 1990),
p. 193–201.
The African, Caribbean and Pacific (ACP) states, and particularly the francophone African states, fear that the EC will become preoccupied with its internal concerns, and with European issues, thus pushing them to the margins. In particular they fear a 'fortress Europe' and increased tension as they seek to industrialize. The author argues that 'it is likely that the ACP . . . will be affected only marginally by the trade creating and trade diverting effects of the Single European Market' and that their most likely response will be to seek closer regional integration and mutual trade – in effect an African Common Market – and to look for beneficial links with other international trading blocs.

291 **EC–ACP relations in the 1980s.**
Mike Cooper. *European Access*, 1989, 6 (Dec. 1989), p. 35–43.
Although primarily a review of the literature on this topic, the author also provides a brief, straightforward introduction to the major issues in the relationship with the African, Caribbean and Pacific (ACP) states. References are given to official documents, journal articles and monographs, presenting both the official view of European Community–Third World relations and critiques of official policy. It covers the period from the second Lomé Convention to the opening of negotiations for the fourth (1980–89).

292 **The European Community and the Third World: the Lomé Convention and its impact.**
Ellen Frey-Wouters, foreword by Richard A. Falk. New York: Praeger, 1980. 290p.
Discusses in detail the build-up and the meaning of the Lomé Convention, and in a final chapter looks into the prospects for the late 1980s.

293 **The Lomé Convention in a new international economic order.**
Edited by Frans A. M. Alting von Geusau. Leyden, The Netherlands: Sijthoff, 1977. 249p.
A set of optimistic essays which makes the point that the new features in the Lomé Convention – those which did not exist in the Yaoundé or Arusha Conventions – pave the way for a new beginning for global economic relations.

294 **Trade relations in the EEC: an empirical investigation.**
Mordechai E. Kreinin. New York: Praeger; London: Pall Mall, 1974.
126p.
This book was written and published before the first Lomé Convention was concluded.
Although Lomé did improve the conditions of trade for less developed countries the
author also points out that there was great potential in trade between these countries.

295 **The European Community and the developing world: the role of the**
Lomé Convention.
Marjorie Lister. Aldershot, England: Gower, 1988. 240p.
A useful history of these tortuous negotiations going back to the Yaoundé Conventions
of 1963 and 1969. The author has produced in readable form the vast range of
commercial, economic and financial facts, and the legalistic requirements and
obligations, and she highlights the political and diplomatic nuances which underlie the
Lomé Convention. However, the detailed analysis undertaken here of the Convention's antecedents, its provisions, and its political implications reveals that it was not
the force for change which had been widely supposed.

296 **EEC and the Third World: renegotiating Lomé.**
Edited by Christopher Stevens. London: Hodder & Stoughton, for
Overseas Development Institute and the Institute of Development
Studies, 1984. 198p.
Six authors examine Lomé in action and they raise various queries such as why a larger
proportion of aid funds go to francophone countries than to anglophone ones; why
more use is not made of the Community's delegations in the individual states.

297 **Europe and Africa: from association to partnership.**
Carol Cosgrove Twitchett. Farnborough, England: Saxon House,
1978. 195p.
This is an analysis of how the Lomé Agreement has operated since it was signed in
1975. The author emphasizes the French influence in the development of the
association; indeed, without the French it is unlikely that the idea would have been
included in the Treaty of Rome.

298 **A framework for development: the EEC and the ACP.**
Carol Cosgrove Twitchett. London: Allen & Unwin, 1981. 160p.
A critical survey of the first Lomé Convention which was considered a particularly
important achievement by the European Community but was not so enthusiastically
endorsed by Third World leaders. The book is divided into two parts; the first gives
details of Lomé I and its implementation, while the second examines the problems
arising from the Lomé II negotiations and takes a quick look at the future.

299 **Lomé IV Convention.**
The Courier, no. 120 (March–April 1990). 214p.
This special issue reprints the most recent Lomé Convention which was signed in
December 1989, supporting the text with discussion of its context and a summary of
the evolution of the key points. The main features of Lomé IV, in comparison with its

predecessor are: greater use of EC funds to aid economic restructuring; the opening up of loans and grants for the relief of debt problems; the inclusion of the environment and human rights as important concerns and the promotion of private-sector enterprise and a greater focus on decentralized forms of development co-operation.

Foreign Relations

General

300 Norway and Europe in the 1970s.
Hilary Allen.   Oslo: Universitetsforlaget, 1979. 289p.
The author sets out to answer why the Norwegians rejected membership of the EEC in
the referendum of September 1972, and how Norway's relations with the Community
have developed since then. She explains that the referendum was turned by the anti-
marketeers into a debate on the future of Norwegian society, whilst the EEC's
supporters ran a weak campaign. The book also describes in some detail the
subsequent free-trade agreement between Norway and the Community and the
relationship between the two sides since 1973.

**301 Europe and the Andean countries: a comparison of economic policies
and institutions.**
Edited by Ciro Angarita, Peter Coffey.   London: Pinter, 1988. 200p.
Experts from both sides of the Atlantic examine major areas of mutual economic and
legal interest to Europeans and Latin Americans. Problems are highlighted and an
attempt is made to ascertain whether the EC could serve as a model for Latin
American countries.

302 Organizing Western Europe.
Clive Archer.   Sevenoaks, England: Edward Arnold, 1990. 224p.
This text analyses the major Western European inter-state organizations established
since the Second World War. The aims, membership, activities and structure of these
organizations are examined, alongside the rôles and functions they fulfil in the
international political system. The historical backgrounds to the creation and existence
of the organizations themselves leads to a valuable examination of the creation of the
Single European Market in the European Communities in 1992 and of the changes
experienced by the European allies in the North Atlantic Treaty Organization
(NATO). There is a chapter for each major organization, including the Organization

71

for Economic Co-operation and Development (OECD), the Council of Europe, the European Coal and Steel Community (ECSC), the EEC, the European Free Trade Association (EFTA), and NATO. Because of their importance in the development of the economic and security policies of Western European countries, the European Communities and NATO receive particularly detailed consideration.

303   **The European Community and the world.**
Richard Bailey.   London: Hutchinson, 1973. 200p. bibliog.
This study covers a wide spectrum of EEC external relations. There are detailed analyses of the impact of British membership on Australia, Canada and New Zealand, on the seven members of EFTA, on the USA, and on the countries of the Eastern European bloc.

304   **Mediterranean Europe and the Common Market: studies of economic growth and integration.**
Edited by Eric N. Baklanoff.   Montgomery, Alabama: University of Alabama Press, for the Office of International Studies and Programs, 1977. 244p.
A well-edited collection of essays. On economic growth they are very analytical and stress the common problems of the Mediterranean countries: dependence on agriculture, the export of migrant workers to the EC, the growth of tourism with its seasonal impact on employment. Economic growth will take place but integration will be slow and the EEC can do little to change that pace.

305   **Europe at sixes and sevens: the common market, the free trade association, and the United States.**
Emile Benoit.   New York: Columbia University Press, 1961. 275p.
Half of this book is about the EEC and EFTA, while the other half is about the effect of the Common Market on the United States. The Rome Treaty is competently described. Although there were many changes of groupings during the next few years the basic analysis is sound. The most valuable part of the study is that on the relationship between Europe and the United States, and the competitiveness of American exports is studied in detail. The final chapter describes the implications of European integration, particularly for the Atlantic alliance and the underdeveloped countries. Benoit is pro-European – believing in economic growth, lower tariffs and more aid – and he thinks in terms of an Atlantic union when the EEC has achieved political and economic power.

306   **Implications of the EC internal market for relations with Eastern Europe.**
Klaus Bolz.   *Intereconomics*, vol. 25, no. 1 (Jan.–Feb. 1990), p. 36–43.
An early survey of the EEC's future relations with the newly democratizing countries of the Council for Mutual Economic Assistance (CMEA), in the light of the Single European Market. Bilateral relations with each country are examined, and the author overviews the relationship between the EC and the CMEA as a whole. He argues that relations will necessarily be problematic and that closer integration of individual CMEA members into the EC will be difficult until political problems are resolved. A

possible way forward may be for the CMEA states to join the European Free Trade Association (EFTA) and become associate members of the EC. However, it is felt that in practice this could present as many problems as bilateral relations.

307   **The EEC and Brazil: trade, capital investment and the debt problem.**
Edited by Peter Coffey, Luiz Corrêa do Lago.   London: Pinter, 1988. 200p.

The recent return of Brazil to parliamentary democracy, together with the unrelated but important Brazilian foreign debt, have increased Western interest in Brazil's affairs. In particular, the European Economic Community, as Brazil's principle trading partner and main source of capital investment, is inevitably closely linked with Brazil's destiny. In this book the contributors examine the pattern of trade and investment and the proposed changes for the 1990s.

308   **The external economic relations of the EEC.**
Peter Coffey.   London: Macmillan, 1976. 118p.

A selective (perhaps too selective) study of the external relations of the Community. The pages are dominated by monetary problems and Coffey is particularly good at describing a monetary crisis, but there were/are other problems.

309   **The European Common Market and the world.**
Werner Feld.   Englewood Cliffs, New Jersey: 1967; London: Prentice Hall, 1968. 184p.

This publication is concerned not with Community internal growth but with the Community's impact on the rest of the world.

310   **The external relations of the European Community: perspectives, policies and responses.**
Edited by Frans A. M. Alting von Geusau.   Lexington, Massachusetts; Farnborough, England: Saxon House Heath, for the John F. Kennedy Institute, 1974. 132p.

Based on papers presented to a congress of political scientists in 1973, this book covers EEC relations with the US, the Mediterranean countries, Eastern Europe and China. The editor concludes that improved external relations 'is a problem of internal unification and cohesion'.

311   **Foreign policy actions of the European Community: the politics of scale.**
Roy H. Ginsberg.   London: Adamantine Press, 1989. 190p.

The European Community has taken a surprising number of diverse civilian foreign policy actions that defy easy categorization and explanation. This book traces trends in the development of EC foreign policy activity by tabulating the number and content of joint foreign policy actions from 1958 to 1985.

312 **Little Europe, wider Europe and Western European co-operation.**
Wolfgang Hager. *Journal of Common Market Studies*, vol. 21, nos
1–2 (Sept. 1982), p. 171–89.
A detailed study of the interrelationships of the EC, the US, West Germany,
Organization for Economic Co-operation and Development (OECD) and General
Agreement on Tariffs and Trade (GATT). With particular focus on the EC–EFTA
relationship the author argues that an EC–EFTA area offers an 'optimum trading
area', and examines areas of possible co-operation. He concludes that preferential
trading arrangements must be extended beyond the EC.

313 **External relations of the European Community: associations and trade
agreements.**
Stanley Henig. London: Chatham House and PEP, 1971. 145p.
This study explores the early years of negotiating trade associations and agreements,
especially the association treaty with Greece in 1961.

314 **The European Community and South Africa: European political
co-operation under strain.**
Martin Holland. London: Pinter, 1988. 204p.
This book by the Jean Monnet Fellow, European University Institute, Florence, looks
at the EC's policy towards South Africa during 1977–87. The author deals primarily
with constraints imposed on Community action, which result from the very process
of consensus and co-operation among the twelve member countries.

315 **The EC and changes in Central and Eastern Europe.**
Rudolf Hrbek. *Intereconomics*, vol. 25, no. 3 (May–June 1990),
p. 131–9.
Written as the EC was in the process of formulating its responses to the massive
changes in the former Eastern Bloc; the author examines the broad implications for the
EC of these changes. Given only finite resources, EC development aid to Central and
Eastern Europe must come at the expense of aid to other areas, principally the
Mediterranean and developing world. In effect this will mean a change in the EC's
centre of gravity, especially as the rôle of Germany in EC affairs will increase. Set
against this is the possibility that these new demands will act as a spur to greater
integration, and the overall decline in the importance of military power in Europe will
place greater emphasis on economic and political power, which the author feels will
work to the Community's advantage.

316 **Europe 1992: an American perspective.**
Edited by Gary Clyde Hufbauer. Washington, DC: Brookings
Institution, 1990. 406p.
This book analyses and gives pragmatic advice on the likely impact of the Single
European Act 1992 on the United States. It studies four main areas: automobiles,
financial services, semiconductors and telecommunications. The consensus seems to be
that those US firms already established in Europe should face few difficulties but warns
that some battles with loud rhetoric and some retaliation may take place from time to
time. Aimed at an American readership it provides, in the appendices, much useful
reference material on the EC.

317 **Norway and the European Community.**
Aneurin Rhys Hughes. *European Access*, 1990, 2 (April), p. 8–10.
Describes Norway's relationship with the EC before and after the 1972 referendum
when Norway rejected membership of the Community. By 1989 relationships had
improved, following a speech on EC–EFTA relationship by EC President Delors.

318 **EEC policy towards Eastern Europe.**
Edited by Ieuan G. John. Lexington, Massachusetts; London: Heath,
1975. 148p.
This collection of papers was originally prepared for a conference sponsored by the
International Politics Department of the University College of Wales, Aberystwyth in
1973. An interesting historical survey, but weak on the 'crystal ball'.

319 **A nation writ large? Foreign-policy problems before the European
Community.**
Edited by Max Kohnstamm, Wolfgang Hager. London: Macmillan,
1973. 275p.
A very early series of studies on the development of a 'common foreign policy'.

320 **European economic integration and the United States.**
Lawrence B. Krause. Washington, DC: Brookings Institution, 1968.
265p. bibliog.
An intelligent analysis of the extent to which EFTA and the EEC have promoted trade
creation, trade diversion and income growth.

321 **The European Community and New Zealand.**
Juliet Lodge. London: Pinter, 1982. 249p.
New Zealand maintained a special access to the British market for dairy and lamb
exports after Britain's accession to the European Community and this book explains
how this was achieved. This case-study will be of general interest to those concerned
with the external relations of the EC.

322 **The Common Market: friend or competitor?**
Jesse W. Markham, Charles E. Fiero, Howard S. Piquet, foreword by
John H. Prime. New York University Press, for the School of
Commerce, Accounts and Finance, 1964. 123p. (The Charles C.
Moskowitz Lectures, no. IV).
These three lectures, delivered in New York, were aimed at an intelligent but
uninstructed American audience. Professor Markham deals with the progress of
competition policy, Charles E. Fiero assesses the economic consequences of US
investment in Europe, and Howard S. Piquet compares the EEC economy with that of
the USA. All lecturers were fair-minded and optimistic for the future.

323 **The unfinished story: Turkish labour migration to Western Europe, with special reference to the Federal Republic of Germany.**
P. L. Martin. Geneva: International Labour Office, 1991. 200p.

This book traces the movement of Turkish migrants to EC countries over the last thirty years. Drawing on both published research and on the testimonies of key informants, it examines the economic and social impacts on both Turkey and the Federal Republic of Germany, and asks whether there might be further large-scale migration if Turkey became a member of the European Communities.

324 **The great debate: New Zealand, Britain and the EEC, the shaping of attitudes.**
Robert McLuskie. Wellington, New Zealand: Decision Research Centre, Victoria University of Wellington in association with the (New Zealand) Institute of International Affairs, 1986. 175p.

A detailed study of Britain's progress towards membership of the EEC and its implications for New Zealand. It draws heavily upon parliamentary debates and media reports and on the author's experience of working for several New Zealand agricultural bodies.

325 **The European Community and Latin America: a case study in global expansion.**
A. Glenn Mower, Jr. Westport, Connecticut; London: Greenwood, 1982. 180p.

Aimed at an American readership, this book attempts to explain that the European Community is an emerging world force which will necessarily develop a significant relationship with Latin America. The author backs his arguments with a bombardment of statistics.

326 **The European Community and the international trading system. Vol. 1: completing the Uruguay round of GATT.**
Anna Murphy. Brussels: Centre for European Policy Studies Publications, 1990. 166p.

This volume deals with the relationship between the EC and the Uruguay Round of trade negotiations in the General Agreement on Tariffs and Trade (GATT) which was to have been concluded in December 1990. A second volume will follow. The study is largely a political analysis but it deals adequately with all the problems on the negotiating agenda.

327 **Eastern Europe and the European Community: a study in trade relations.**
Susan Senior Nello. Hemel Hempstead, England: Harvester Wheatsheaf, 1991. 256p.

The single market programme of the European Community was gaining momentum in the late 1980s as political reforms were sweeping through Eastern Europe. One of the consequences of the new-found cohesion amongst Community members during that period was a fresh look at trade relations and this was given added urgency by the reforms in Eastern Europe. In the first part of the book, Susan Nello describes and assesses the trade arrangements in place prior to the 1988–89 watershed in European affairs, and analyses the trade patterns between the two blocs. In the second part, she deals with the reforms in Eastern Europe and their implications for trade relations with the Community. She reviews the reforms, including Western measures to aid the process, and also considers German unification, before going on to evaluate the potential for new forms of integration and association in Europe, and the prospects for East–West inter-firm co-operation and joint ventures.

328 **Turkey in Europe and Europe in Turkey.**
Turgut Özal. London: Rustem & Brother, 1991. 375p.
An interesting study of Turkey by its president. A large part of the book is Turkish history up to the time of Atatürk but the Europeanization of Turkey leading to the request for membership of the European Community makes for interesting and informative reading.

329 **Economic diplomacy between the European Community and Japan 1959–1981.**
Albrecht Rothacher. Aldershot, England: Gower, 1973. 377p.
This work focuses on Euro-Japanese problems for a particular period and also gives a wide survey of the subject. Much factual information has been assimilated and utilized but perhaps there are too many footnotes for easy reading (Chapter 6, for example, has 580!).

330 **The EEC and the Mediterranean countries.**
Edited by Avi Shlaim, G. N. Yannapoulos. London: Cambridge University Press, 1976. 352p.
Analyses the piecemeal way in which agreements have been reached with Mediterranean countries.

331 **Are EC–Japan–US relations at the crossroads?**
Radha Singha. *Intereconomics*, vol. 25, no. 5 (Sept.–Oct., 1990), p. 229–37.
The Uruguay Round of multi-lateral trade negotiations pinpointed that closer integration of the EC, in effect the creation of a European economy, presented a threat to US–Japanese dominance of the world economy, and has created fears of a 'Fortress Europe'. Both Japan and the US pressed for rival free trade areas in Oceania and the Americas, and the author examines, issue by issue, the main areas of tension, including textiles, dumping and intellectual property.

332 **Europe and the Caribbean.**
Edited by Paul Sutton. London: Macmillan, 1990. 260p.
Columbus arrived in the West Indies in 1492 and this publication is to commemorate the 500th anniversary of that European contact. The initial papers are on the British, French and Dutch involvement in that area, while later papers deal with the Spanish and Soviet influence. It then goes on to examine the influence of Latin American countries. The conclusion reached is that European influence in the Caribbean will depend on the goodwill of the United States.

333 **The European Communities as an actor in international society.**
Paul Taylor. *Journal of European Integration*, vol. 6, no. 1 (Fall 1982), p. 7–42.

The author examines in detail the widest aspects of EC external relations including the rôle of the institutions and the relationship between Community foreign policy and that of individual member states. He argues that the Commission lacks the necessary executive competence to represent the EC in foreign policy, having to work closely in co-ordination with member states. Taylor argues that the background unity necessary for a truly EC foreign policy stance is missing.

334 **Relations between the European Community and Turkey.**
Nahit Töre. *European Access*, 1990, 3 (June), p. 8–11.

September 1963 saw the signing of the agreement between the EC and Turkey, following the declared wish of Turkey in June 1959 that it should become an associate member. Progress to full membership has had many setbacks but the formal application for full membership was presented to the Council in April 1987. This article analyses the prospects for success.

335 **Europe and the world: the external relations of the Common Market.**
Edited by Kenneth J. Twitchett. London: Europa, for the David Davies Memorial Institute of International Studies, 1976. 210p.

An edited series of essays on the EEC and its relationships with the USA, the Mediterranean, the ACP countries, Eastern Europe, and the Third World. It poses questions about what progress will be made when more members join the Community.

336 **1992 and the non-EC countries: the corporate consequences of the European internal market.**
Daniel Venter. Chichester, England: Carden, 1990. 350p.

1992 will have far-reaching implications for countries outside the European Community. This book looks at these implications and provides non-EC businesses with an effective means to prepare for the challenges of 1 January 1993.

337 **Comecon, trade and the West.**
William V. Wallace, Roger A. Clarke. London: Pinter, 1986. 176p.

A short analysis of Comecon and East–West economic relations. It is good on history but, understandably, shaky on predictions. However, East–West trade will rapidly increase, with or without Comecon, and this book provides useful background material.

338 **Austria and the EC.**
T. Wieser, E. Kitymantel. *Journal of Common Market Studies*, vol. 28, no. 4 (June 1990), p. 432–49.

The authors present a detailed historical survey of Austria's relations with the EC since the 1950s and review the consequences of the Single Market for the Austrian economy and that country's membership of EFTA. They conclude that 1992 has put pressure on Austrian politics, its economy and institutions. Many in Austria expect benefits from EC membership – especially in terms of their government's microeconomic policy –

and there is little fear of discrimination against Austria. Participation in the European Economic Space is favoured by many; they feel that free movement of capital and services can be particularly beneficial and they stress the importance for Austria of harmonization and standardization.

339 **The European Common Market and its meaning to the United States. A statement of national policy by the Research and Policy Committee.**
Committee for Economic Development, with a foreword by T. V. Houser. New York; Toronto; London: McGraw Hill, 1959. 151p.
An informative report stressing the need for a realistic philosophy which would 'provide guiding principles to judge the rights and wrongs of departures from multilateral non-discriminating world commerce and finance'.

340 **Report by the EC Directorate to the Prime Minister and Minister of Foreign Affairs regarding Malta's membership of the European Community.**
Valletta, Malta: Department of Information, 1990. 381p.
This report explains what membership would mean for the political, economic and social structure of Malta. In addition, it is a valuable text on procedures within the EC, particularly on the legislative, political and social processes.

European Free Trade Association (EFTA)

341 **The politics of change: EFTA and the Nordic countries' responses to the EC in the early 1990s.**
Clive Church. *Journal of Common Market Studies*, vol. 28, no. 4 (June 1990), p. 402–27.
Clive Church examines the background to EC–EFTA–Scandinavian relations, and details each Scandinavian country's own relations with the two bodies. He finds that EFTA countries are being forced to think of their relationships in political rather than purely economic terms, and examines the tensions over independence and neutrality that this is causing. His conclusion is that '1992' and its implications may force a long hard re-examination of the Scandinavian states' national identities.

342 **Assessing the effects of EC integration on EFTA countries: the position of Norway and Sweden.**
Jan I. Haarland. *Journal of Common Market Studies*, vol. 28, no. 4 (June 1990), p. 379–400.
A detailed case-study of the possible effects of '1992' on the two largest non-EC countries of Western Europe. Although the main focus is on trade, valuable consideration is given to the wider effects of the Single Market. The author concludes that freer international trade may benefit smaller, open economies, but that any gains

will depend on structural flexibility and internal trade policies. Direct participation in EC integration may be the easiest way to achieve the internal political action needed if benefits are to be realized.

343 **EEC–EFTA: more than just good friends?**
Edited by J. Jamar, H. Wallace.   Bruges, Belgium: College of Europe, 1988. 374p.

A report of a conference held at Bruges. The editors hold the view that 'an experiment in living together has been made, with a decision about marriage later'. Other contributors are more sceptical although one states that 'several EFTA countries are more integrated with the Community than most Community members'.

344 **EFTA: the problems of an all-European role.**
Iver B. Neumann.   *Journal of Common Market Studies*, vol. 28, no. 4 (June 1990), p. 359–77.

EFTA must act to find a rôle for itself in pan-European politics if it is not to be acted upon. The author examines the possible rôles EFTA might play on the European stage as the EC, European Political Co-operation and the reviving Western European Union (WEU) come to be the focus of pan-European thinking, and as the CMEA dissolves, opening wide questions about relations with Eastern Europe and about the East–West dialogue within Europe. He points to two main rôles for EFTA: that of a buffer between the Soviet Union and the EC, and as an 'ante-chamber' to hold prospective EC members whilst their economies gain momentum.

345 **EFTA in the 1990s: the search for a new identity.**
Phillipe G. Niel.   *Journal of Common Market Studies*, vol. 28, no. 4 (June 1990), p. 327–58.

The author examines the challenges facing EFTA in the 1990s, concluding that its new rôle will in all probability be determined by the institutional framework of the EC–EFTA European Economic Space (EES). Niel identifies three main areas of threat: the Single European Market, a development impossible for EFTA to parallel because of its institutional and legislative character; new technology, requiring high research and development expenditure and threatening traditional industries; the growth of the EC as a world power, another development whose basis EFTA cannot match. To support this, the article gives a detailed analysis of EFTA–EC trade and of EFTA's rôle in the world economy. The author concludes that although EFTA can perform a useful function as a route towards integration for those economies for whom EC membership would be impossible in the short term, there is a real danger that EFTA members will have no option but to join the EC.

346 **The wider western Europe: EC policy towards the EFTA countries.**
Thomas Pedersen.   London: Royal Institute of International Affairs, 1988. 44p.

An important discussion paper which should be read in conjunction with Helen Wallace's book *The wider Western Europe: reshaping the EC/EFTA relationship* (q.v.).

347 **The wider western Europe: reshaping the EC/EFTA relationship.**
Edited by Helen Wallace. London: Pinter, for Royal Institute of
International Affairs, 1991. 285p.

The European Free Trade Association (EFTA), consisting of Austria, Finland,
Iceland, Norway, Sweden, Switzerland and soon to be joined by Liechtenstein, is
searching for a method of having closer links with the European Communities. This
becomes even more important as Eastern European countries are interested in new
alignments. Obviously negotiations leading to any agreement are going to be difficult,
but especially so where agriculture is concerned. Also EFTA, as a free trade area, will
wish to avoid being caught in the Brussels web of control.

348 **The European Community, EFTA and the New Europe.**
Journal of Common Market Studies, vol. 28, no. 4 (June 1990). 197p.

The relationship between the two free trade areas of Western Europe are examined in
the academic essays in this special issue. Articles cover the implications of an
integrating EC and democratizing East on EFTA, on EFTA–EC relations, and on the
relationships between Scandinavia and Austria and the Community.

Common Agricultural and Fisheries Policy

Agriculture

349 Combinable crops and the EC.
Mary Abbott.   Blackwell Scientific, 1990. 128p.

This National Farmers' Union handbook is a comprehensive guide to the intricacies of the European Community and the Common Agricultural Policy as it affects cereals and other combinable crops. It is aimed at farmers, traders and advisers. It is a useful reference on all aspects of EC structures and decision-making processes, together with an explanation of the complexities of the price support arrangements.

350 Tensions in the U.S.–E.E.C. relations: the agriculture issue.
Richard Butler, Thomas Saylor.   Washington, DC: National Planning Association, 1986. 42p.

Two experts examine the long-standing dispute between the United States and the European Community over policies affecting agricultural trade. The report also records a discussion among members of the British–North American Committee of this conflict, exacerbated by the accession of Spain and Portugal to the EC and by US agricultural legislation.

351 The Common Agricultural Policy in the 1980s.
Mike Cooper.   *European Access*, 1989, 2 (April 1989), p. 46–55.

Primarily a survey of the official and academic literature on the subject, this article also provides a clear introduction to the structures, issues and debates for a lay audience. Cooper discusses the traditional mechanisms of the Common Agricultural Policy, the reforms of the late 1980s, and the growing importance of social and 'green' issues.

352 **The food and farm policies of the European Community.**
Simon Harris, Alan Swinbank, Guy Wilkinson. Chichester, England;
New York: John Wiley & Sons, 1983. 354p.

A comprehensive account of how the Common Agricultural Policy (CAP) operated in the late 1970s. The authors have considerable experience in commerce and government and aim to give guidance to businessmen and others who require an understanding of its complexities. The book shows the importance of the CAP to the food industries and in turn their importance to the CAP. It also considers the impact of CAP policies on third countries.

353 **Reappraising the Common Agricultural Policy for the 1990s.**
Gisela Hendriks. *European Research*, vol. 1, pt 6 (Nov. 1990),
p. 1–5.

The purpose of this article is to reappraise the profile of the Common Agricultural Policy (CAP) in the Community of the 1990s. After a brief historical overview of the CAP's main developments, the effectiveness of recent reform measures is examined in an attempt to assess whether a major change in the method of agricultural support has taken place in the Community. The author believes that the CAP has reached a turning point and it is time to take stock.

354 **In search of the CAP's agricultural community.**
Berkley Hill. *Journal of Agricultural Economics*, vol. 41, no. 3 (Sept. 1990), p. 316–26.

The Common Agricultural Policy (CAP) is designed to increase overall welfare in the EC by targeting agricultural incomes for support – but who actually benefits? In a stimulating contribution to the academic debate on the CAP, the author, from Wye College, argues that if the EC does not produce a more rigorous definition of the groups intended to benefit from the CAP it will be impossible to analyse its actual effects or to produce genuine improvements. He suggests that the EC Statistical Office's definition, which includes any household where self-employment in agriculture is the chief source of income, may be as useful as any.

355 **The Common Market and world agriculture: trade patterns in temperate-zone foodstuffs.**
Francis Knox. New York: Praeger; London: Pall Mall, 1972. 138p.

Written before the start of negotiations to enlarge the Community, this study traces the tendency of high-cost producers to increase their market share by enjoying the protection of agricultural policies. It is a rather narrow approach which ignores many of the other problems which would occur as a result of changes in trade in agricultural products.

356 **Agricultural policy and the Common Market.**
John Marsh, Christopher Ritson. London: PEP and Chatham House, 1971. 199p.

A handbook about the Common Agricultural Policy (CAP) as it stood in 1970, and a highly critical economic analysis of that policy. It also contains two large appendices with statistical and other data. They put forward three ways of dealing with the CAP. 'The first scheme assures no departure in the CAP, but rather a gradual evolution matching the developing problems of surplus production and low incomes. The second retains the notion that income support must be distributed in return for production through a system of high prices, but seeks to prevent surpluses by quotas and by a Community price designed to allow further increments in output only when these do not require excessive Community support. The last scheme abandons the notion of supporting incomes through prices, whilst providing income support and a variety of incentives to mobility'. The authors tend to favour the third method.

357   **Agricultural policy reform: politics and process in the EC and USA.**
H. Wayne Moyer, Timothy E. Josling.   Hemel Hempstead, England:
Harvester Wheatsheaf, 1990. 256p.

The formation of agricultural policy, and particularly its reform, is a very contentious issue both within the EC and USA and also in relations between the two countries. Many of the reports and studies which have investigated the issues have focused on narrow technical details of the reform process. The authors offer a much-needed alternative perspective by examining the rôle of the political process in explaining agricultural policy decisions.

358   **French agriculture and the political integration of western Europe.**
Hanns Peter Muth.   Leyden, The Netherlands: Sijthoff, 1970. 320p.
bibliog.

A study basically concerned with the French peasants and their response to the Common Agricultural Policy. Because of disillusionment with French national agricultural policy the agricultural unions embraced the CAP, not so much because of political idealism, but to avoid national erosion of material benefits.

359   **The Common Agricultural Policy: prospects for change.**
Joan Pearce.   London: Routledge & Kegan Paul, for the Royal
Institute of International Affairs, 1981. 122p.

A short study of intervention or non-intervention to balance supply and demand in agricultural products. The author argues that intervention is strongest in the short run and weakest in the long.

360   **Wheat, Europe and GATT: a political economy analysis.**
Peter W. B. Phillips.   London: Pinter, 1990. 272p.

Throughout the 1970s EC wheat price policy concentrated on supporting farm incomes, which neither permitted nor required an active external policy. In the 1980s, however, prices were increasingly directed by market conditions. Shifts in the structures surrounding the wheat system had weakened the pan-European farm lobby. A patchwork of new agreements evolved between policy-makers, commodity groups and non-farm lobbies, to support an active, rather than a defensive, export policy. In this study, the author examines the implications of this new export orientation for the rest of the world via the Uruguay Round of the GATT.

361   **The Common Agricultural Policy and the world economy.**
Edited by C. Ritson, D. Harvey.   Wallingford, England: CAB
International, 1990. 300p.

Provides an up-to-date overview of the origins, development and current problems of
the CAP of the European Community.

362   **The politics of agriculture in the European Community.**
Edmund Neville-Rolfe.   London: Policy Studies Institute, 1984. 547p.

The book takes us up to, but does not include, 1984, a year which was a watershed in
the development of the Common Agricultural Policy (CAP). Neville-Rolfe explains
that many of the problems that kept the CAP in the headlines over the years were
recognized as far back as the Strese Conference of 1958. He explodes the myth that
France did not have the highest level of agricultural support among the Six and
pressure for greater protection came mainly from the Federal Republic of Germany.
He maintains that the initial over-generous support for cereals is a main cause of many
of the CAP's later problems. The second half of the book analyses the annual price
reviews.

363   **The Common Agricultural Policy of the European Community:**
principles and consequences.
Edited by Julius Rosenblatt.   Washington, DC: International
Monetary Fund, 1988. 70p. (Occasional Papers, 62).

A short but important pamphlet setting out exactly what is given in the title.

364   **Prospects for the European food system.**
Bruce Traill.   Barking, England: Elsevier Science Publishers, 1989.
250p.

This book is based on reports prepared for the EC Commission's directorate-general
for development as part of the Forecasting and Assessment in Science and Technology
(FAST) programme. It offers a unique European perspective on future changes in the
food industry from the technological as well as the consumer angle.

365   **Agriculture: the cost of joining the Common Market.**
T. K. Warley.   London: Chatham House and PEP, 1967. 57p.

This pamphlet is a model of conciseness and lucidity and many of the suggestions made
were adopted by the UK government.

366   **Agriculture, the Commonwealth and E.E.C.**
London: Political and Economic Planning, 1961. 61p.

This pamphlet is concerned with the agricultural policies of Britain and the European
Economic Community and how they can be reconciled. The first part contains an
account of the state of the debate inside the Community on devising a common
agricultural policy. Following a brief sketch of the British system of agricultural
protection, there follows an analysis of the impact on agricultural policy with the UK
as a full member. British agricultural interests are examined and the difficult issue of
the continuance of free entry for temperate foodstuffs from the Commonwealth is
rightly identified. The pamphlet produces no solutions but is an excellent
contribution to greater understanding of the problems.

367 **A Common Agricultural Policy for the 1990s.**
Luxembourg: Office for Official Publications of the European
Communities, 1989. 80p. (*European Documentation* 5/1989).

The European Community's own guide to the reformed CAP. In common with all this
series it takes a positive but clear-headed view of the subject. The text is
straightforward and accessible, supported where appropriate with statistics and
diagrams.

368 **The future of rural society.**
Luxembourg: Office for Official Publications of the European
Communities, 1988. 87p. (Commission Working Documents COM (88)
501).

A seminal paper essential to the understanding of the future course of the Common
Agricultural Policy reform and regional policy. The Commission seeks to draw
together all the current strands of social and structural policy in a rural context, putting
forward a policy which will not just support existing structures, but which will promote
adaptation. The four main pillars of the new-style rural (as opposed to farm/price)
policy will be: the promotion of conservation and environmental protection; promotion
of service industries; a less passive aid policy; promotion of rural infrastructure,
education and training.

The agricultural situation in the Community.
See item no. 557.

Information on agriculture.
See item no. 574.

Fisheries

369 **European integration and the common fisheries policy.**
Michael Leigh. London; Canberra: Croom Helm, 1983. 228p.

On 25 January 1983 the Council of Ministers of the EC approved regulations
establishing a common fisheries policy. The conflict for access to fishing grounds is a
very live issue and this book is a generally cautious, straightfaced record of events. It is
written by an official of the Community and so does not attempt to answer the question
of the future of the fishing industry and whether the common fisheries policy provides
the prospect of growth, or simply managed decline.

370 **The Common Fisheries Policy of the European Community.**
M. Wise. London; New York: Methuen, 1984. 200p.

This useful description of the fisheries policy also contains the important parts of the
main fisheries policy regulation. There are useful geographical definitions and
statistical tables.

Law

371 Competition law.
J. H. Agnew. London: George Allen & Unwin, 1985. 240p. bibliog.
The rapid growth of legislation in recent years in the anti-trust field has given competition law renewed importance as firms strive to capture and consolidate their share of the market in the face of ever-increasing competition from foreign multinationals. In this book, the author provides a clear, concise introduction to competition law and anti-trust legislation as Western economies seek to promote a competitive business environment. The book presents an up-to-date view of anti-trust policy in the United Kingdom, United States and West Germany, and gives examples of how the practices of a single firm affect competition: merger activity; and tacit collusion between enterprises.

372 European community law and organizational development.
Andrew W. Axline. Dobbs Ferry, New York: Oceana, 1968. 214p. bibliog.
A study of the changes necessary to bring about integrated national and community law.

373 Legal problems of an enlarged European Community.
Edited by M. E. Bathurst, K. R. Simmonds, N. March Hunnings, Jane Welch. London: Stevens & Sons, for the British Institute of International and Comparative Law, 1972. 369p. (British Institute Studies in International and Comparative Law, no. 6).
These are the working papers of a conference held in Dublin in 1970 under the auspices of the British Institute of International and Comparative Law. They deal in a general way with the problems facing those countries wishing to join the European Communities and also those of the states intending to remain outside the Communities.

374 **Judicial control of the European Communities.**
Gerherd Babr.   London: Stevens, for the London Institute of World
Affairs, 1962. 268p. bibliog.

A detailed study of the objectives and powers of the Communities. It explains that the
Treaties lay down the blueprints but the interpretation of the clauses and the actions of
the Commission and the Courts established the true shape of the Communities.

375 **Common Market law of competition.**
C. W. Bellamy, G. D. Child.   London: Sweet & Maxwell, 1987.
3rd ed. 874p.

It is widely acknowledged that competition policy is central to the development of the
European Economic Community. As such, it has proved to be one of the fastest
growing areas of Community law, producing a vast range of legislative and case law
material and making a clear and accurate guide indispensable. The much-expanded
third edition retains the clarity that was the hallmark of previous editions. After an
introductory chapter outlining the relevant provisions of the EEC treaty and
Community legislation, the contents proceed with an in-depth analysis of the
provisions of Articles 85 and 86, and other relevant articles, special attention being
given to: collaboration in research, development and production, especially in joint
ventures; distribution agreements of all kinds; intellectual property rights; abuse of
dominant position; mergers and acquisitions; notification and its effects; civil remedies;
enforcement and procedure; special sectors; and state aids. The selection of topics
demonstrates the importance attached by the authors to the special interests of private
practitioners and company lawyers on both procedural and substantive aspects. The
text is supported by 31 appendices setting out the relevant articles of the treaty,
regulations, directives and notices, together with full citations of decisions of both the
Community Court and Commission. This is an essential work for anyone concerned
with EEC competition law.

376 **Anti-dumping and anti-subsidy law: the European Communities.**
H. F. Beseler, A. N. Williams.   London: Sweet & Maxwell, 1986.
438p.

The authors examine the interpretation and application of the anti-dumping and anti-
subsidy laws in the EEC in the light of the relevant GATT codes in this area. To
illustrate the approach adopted on specific issues, comparison is made with the
practices of the Community's major trading partners such as the USA and Canada. In
addition, the book breaks new ground by dealing with the current attempts to obtain
through GATT an international consensus on the way anti-subsidy law should be
applied in specific circumstances. The rôle of the Commission of the European
Communities is crucial, first in drafting the rules and procedures and subsequently in
interpreting them, as well as in investigating alleged breaches of the rules and making
member states account for their actions. Dr Beseler, who has worked in the
Directorate-General for External Relations in the Commission and who has been
responsible for Community policy and practice in anti-dumping and anti-subsidy law
from the outset, has had access to the most pertinent documentation in the preparation
of this book.

377   **Lawyers in Europe Companion.**
      Bill Blackburn, Eleanor Sharpston, foreword by Ole Due.
      London: Professional and Business Information, 1990. 150p.
A quick-reference directory for easy access to all judicial, institutional and professional legal bodies in Europe.

378   **Competition policy and merger control in the Single European Market.**
      Leon Brittan.   Cambridge, England: Grotius, 1991. 70p.
What is the jurisdictional basis for the operation of EC competition rules? What is the scope and range of application of the recently adopted 'merger regulation'? These questions are central to the administration of EC competition policy and to any corporate strategic planning in Europe. In two lectures delivered in February 1990 at the University of Cambridge, Sir Leon Brittan examines these problems in the context of the unfolding Single Market. Lecture 1 focuses on the background to and basis of Community jurisdiction in this field. Lecture 2 discusses in some detail the scope of application of the 'merger regulation'. These lectures will be of interest to lawyers, corporate financiers and company strategists alike. For those unfamiliar with the subject matter, the lectures serve as a clear and simple introduction; for those already well versed in this area, they provide an invaluable insight into the thinking of those directly responsible for the implementation of policies.

379   **Free movement in European Community law.**
      F. Burrows.   Oxford: Clarendon Press, 1987. 345p.
Although this book produces nothing new in the way of analysis it is an extremely useful reference tool, giving details of EC law and the free movement of goods, people and capital.

380   **The EEC convention on jurisdiction and the enforcement of judgments.**
      Peter Byrne.   Dublin: Irish Academic Press, 1990. 300p.
In 1968, members of the EEC signed a new international Convention which automatically applied to all legal proceedings of an international character within the Community. It provided that, irrespective of nationality, people residing in the territory of one member country come under the jurisdiction of that state. This book is a thorough analysis of the text of the 1968 Convention, and includes interpretations of fifty-seven judgments which had been made up to the time of going to press.

381   **Common Market law.**
      Alan Campbell, foreword by Lord Denning.   London: Longmans;
      New York: Oceana, 1969. 2 vols.
To provide a definitive reference work on Common Market law in two volumes is a worthy aim. Volume one contains explanations of the law; its nine chapters cover community law, agriculture, restrictive trading agreements, industrial property, transport, the court of justice, association with EEC, accession, external trade agreements, reciprocal enforcement of judgments, mutual recognition of companies, and the European company. There is also a table of regulations and a subject index of regulations. Volume two gives an annotated text of the Treaty of Rome, followed by forty-one appendices. It is an ambitious work but the target audience must be limited to those specializing in Common Market law; others needing information on such matters as agriculture or transport would probably turn to a more specialized work.

382 **European company law.**
C. & L. Belmont.   London: Financial Times Business Information,
1989. 233p.

This edition attempts to detail all the EC attempts to solve the many problems in
company law. It explains the main points concerning the laws and regulations of
individual member states and provides a checklist of the main points for each one. A
new section has been added for each of the European Free Trade Association (EFTA)
member states. The report provides the information on social affairs, taxation, stock
exchange and competition legislation necessary to operate effectively within the EC. It
also summarizes each EC directive or other instrument, proposal or working paper
relevant to company law issues, and gives a statement on implementation (if adopted)
with individual commentaries on those still under discussion. C. & L. Belmont is the
Brussels-based firm of Coopers & Lybrand (International) which provides specialist
advice on the development of EC affairs.

383 **European Law Review.**
Edited by Alan Dashwood, Robin White.   London: Sweet & Maxwell,
1976– . bi-monthly.

The *European Law Review* is a major source for those who need to know what is
happening and how their conduct of affairs will have to be altered. It covers the impact
and effect of the European Community treaties and the resultant legislation, the
consequent alteration of the national law of each of the member states, and the
ensuing changes in the legal relations of those countries with states outside the
European Communities. The *Review* incorporates regular coverage of the European
Communities member states and the Council of Europe.

384 **European company laws.**
Edited by Robert Drury, Peter Xuereb.   Aldershot, England:
Dartmouth Publishing Company, 1991. 350p.

A useful comparative study of company laws in the member states of the EC.

385 **Community law through the cases.**
Neil Elles, assisted by J. H. Vallatt, foreword by Lord Wilberforce.
London: Stevens; New York: Matthew Bender, 1973. 411p.

This study aims 'to provide a guide to the case law of the European Economic
Communities for the busy practitioner, the eager student and the general reader'.
Certainly the first two groups will find it valuable. It provides the text, clause by clause,
of both the EEC and the European Coal and Steel Community (ECSC) treaties and
indicates, with summaries, pertinent court decisions relating to them.

386 **A guide to United Kingdom and European Community competition
policy.**
Nick Gardner.   London: Macmillan, 1991. 228p.

The first book on competition policy to be written primarily for use by British
executives. It covers all activities of the competition authorities of the UK and the EC
over the past ten years.

387   **The foundations of European Community law: an introduction to the constitutional and administrative law of the European Community.**
T. C. Hartley.   Oxford: Clarendon Press, 1981. 551p.
bibliog. (Clarendon Law Series).

A systematic textbook on the body of law of the European Community, which is distinct from the national law of the member states on the one hand, and international law on the other. The Federal Republic of Germany, like the other members of the European Community, has limited its sovereignty, in favour of the Community legal order. The law of the Community takes precedence over German law in certain cases and affects German legislation in many others. For a brief orientation, see Richard Plender, *A practical introduction to European Community law* (London: Sweet & Maxwell, 1980), which includes a bibliography and tables of treaties, of legislation, and of cases brought to the Court of Justice of the European Communities.

388   **Law and institutions of the European Communities.**
D. Lasok, J. W. Bridge.   London: Butterworths, 1987. 4th ed. 513p.

This is a popular student text. It deals with the historical background, institutions, structure and general principles of law in the EC. The relationship between Community law and the law of member states is fully discussed.

389   **Conflict of law in the European Community.**
D. Lasok, P. A. Stone.   Abingdon, England: Professional Books, 1987. 460p.

The book aims to examine the basis of the Community conflicts system and to evaluate the developments up to 1986. The first part is devoted to generalities and the second to a detailed and critical analysis of specialist conventions designed to grapple with the most pressing practical problems. It is aimed at both academics and lawyers in practice.

390   **Competition policy in the European Community: the rules in theory and practice.**
D. L. McLachlan, D. Swann.   London; New York; Toronto: Oxford University Press, for the Royal Institute of International Affairs, 1967. 482p. bibliog.

The first part deals with the adjustments that national governments have made on joining the Community; part two shows how the articles in the treaties have been applied and worked out in practice.

391   **A guide to European Community law.**
P. S. R. F. Mathijsen.   London: Sweet & Maxwell, 1990. 5th ed. 343p. bibliog.

In this compact guide to an increasingly complex area of the law, Professor Mathijsen gives the reader who has little or no previous knowledge of the subject an overall view and understanding of European Community law. There is a brief historical introduction to the European treaties and an outline of the political circumstances surrounding their signing in the 1950s. Also, in the early chapters the functioning of the institutions and organs of the Community are described with, for example, sections on direct elections to and the workings of the European Parliament. Whilst Euratom and the European Coal and Steel Community (ECSC) are covered, the core of the book is devoted to a lively description of the commentary on EEC policies and European case law as they affect a wide range of social, political and commercial issues.

392 **A brief and practical guide to EC law.**
David Medhurst.   Oxford: Blackwell, 1990. 144p.
A quick guide to EC law, aimed at the lawyer who is in a hurry to get a grasp of the subject.

393 **Encyclopedia of competition law.**
Edited by Robert Merkin, Karen Williams, Geoffrey Harding, Jeremy Philips.   London: Sweet & Maxwell, 1987. (Loose-leaf vol.).
The existing sources are numerous and diverse, often crossing defined subject boundaries, making it a difficult task to check quickly and accurately a point covering the UK and EEC competition rules. This work collates and consolidates all these sources in a single loose-leaf volume and includes: UK legislation and regulations; relevant articles of the EEC treaty; EEC directives, notices and regulations; official practice pointers; summaries of leading cases, decisions and reports emanating from various UK and EEC authorities empowered to deal with competition matters; and a short introduction and history of the legislation by the editors to make its development more comprehensible. Annotated in detail throughout and comprehensively cross-referenced, this encyclopaedia allows the user to assess the legality of an agreement or practice from every possible angle, including the likely response of the enforcement authorities. It will be invaluable to practitioners, in-house commercial lawyers, and anyone concerned with this vast subject. The loose-leaf format allows for regular up-dating releases which keep subscribers abreast of all the latest developments. Robert Merkin is Director of Research at Richards Butler and co-author of *Competition law: Anti-trust policy in the UK and the EEC.*

394 **Accounting harmonisation in Europe: towards 1992.**
Christopher Nobes.   London: Financial Times, 1990. 126p.
European accounting practices have changed exceptionally rapidly in recent years, particularly because of changes to law and standards. To understand these changes and to prepare for more, clear insight is needed into the factors that are shaping accounting concepts and practice in an international context. This book identifies the fundamental factors which influence the development of accounting in the EC, examines the practical differences in annual accounts between member states, analyses the laws on financial reporting for companies within the Community, assesses the advantages of and obstacles to harmonization, details the European Commission's harmonization efforts as expressed in its directives on company law, summarizes the effects of these directives on the UK and other countries, and spells out the unresolved problems of accounting harmonization.

395 **Free trade and competition in the EEC: law, policy and practice.**
Helen Papaconstantinou.   London: Routledge, 1988. 256p.
This book examines the extent of free trade within the EEC and attempts to establish the conditions under which a state may operate in the market through the medium of the undertakings which it controls.

396 **Consumer legislation in the EC countries: a comparative analysis.**
Norbert Reich, Hans-W. Micklitz, translated by Sabine Geis.
Wokingham, England; New York: Van Nostrand Reinhold, 1980. 206p.
Prepared for the EC Commission, this study was a first attempt at a comprehensive
analysis of consumer law in the (then) nine EC member countries.

397 **Basic community laws.**
Edited by Bernard Rudden, Derrick Wyatt.   Oxford: Clarendon
Press, 1980. 301p.
The editors aim to present a reference tool for student use which contains 'durable
rules on the fundamental freedoms of the new Europe' and they divide it into: the
Treaties and the related Acts; secondary legislation and other documents; and UK
sources.

398 **The law of the European Economic Community: a commentary on the
EEC Treaty.**
Hans Smit, Peter E. Herzog.   New York: Matthew Bender & Co.,
Columbia Law School Project on European Legal Institutions, 1976.
6 vols.
The work on this commentary was begun in 1967. The result is a systematic article-by-
article examination, in reasonable depth, of all provisions of the Treaty of Rome.

399 **Company law in the UK and the European Community: its
harmonisation and unification.**
Frank Wooldridge.   London: Athlone Press, 1991. 240p.
A clear and up-to-date account of the most important aspects of company law in the
European Community.

400 **An introduction to the law of the European Economic Community.**
Edited by B. A. Wortley.   Manchester, England: Manchester
University Press; Dobbs Ferry, New York: Oceana, 1972. 134p.
The volume contains six lectures delivered at the University of Manchester as part of
the Melland Schill series of lectures. It also contains the White Paper *Legal and
constitutional implications of United Kingdom membership of the European Communities* (Cmnd. 3301).

401 **The law of the Common Market.**
Edited by B. A. Wortley.   Manchester, England: Manchester
University Press; Dobbs Ferry, New York: Oceana, 1974. 248p.
This book takes into consideration the accession of Denmark, Ireland and the United
Kingdom to the Treaty of Rome and extends and expands the information given in *An
introduction to the law of the European Community* published in 1972 and also edited
by B. A. Wortley (q.v.).

402 The substantive law of the EEC.
D. Wyatt, A. Dashwood.   London: Sweet & Maxwell, 1987. 2nd ed. 549p.

Widely acclaimed for its departure from the traditional institutional and jurisdictional approach to the subject and for its concentration on major topics of substantive law, Wyatt and Dashwood's text has proved a major asset to anyone interested in a clear exposition of the economic aspects of European Community law. The second edition presents a completely up-dated analysis of key Community policies in the eminently readable style which distinguished the first edition. Among the areas which have been fully revised to cover the extensive developments in case law and secondary legislation are: free movement of goods; free movement of persons and freedom to provide services; social policy; the Common Agricultural Policy; competition; intellectual property; and public undertakings. Each subject is comprehensively examined, with practical illustrations used to elaborate and explain complex Community regulations – for example, in the field of social security for migrant workers – thereby providing an insight into the fundamental thinking underlying the various policy areas. To complete the coverage there are four introductory chapters outlining the history, aims and characteristics of the Community legal order; these serve to clarify such Community concepts as supremacy, direct applicability, and proportionality.

403 European Community law: an overview.
London: HLT Publications, 1991. 2nd ed. 83p.

The increasing importance of European Community law, with the arrival of the Single European Market in 1992 and Britain's recent entry into the Exchange Rate Mechanism (ERM), makes this invaluable guide a useful addition to European Community handbooks. Its compact and concise format makes it a handy reference work for the business community and the general reader alike, as well as those practising or studying law on a daily basis. The guide examines the various Community institutions and explains the relationship between Community law and British law. It also analyses the sources of Community law, the primacy of Community law, and how the Community law confers rights and duties.

404 Harmonization of company law in the European Community: measures adopted and proposed.
Luxembourg: Office for the Official Publications of the European Communities, 1990. 487p.

This useful publication gives details of action taken on the harmonization of company law in the EC up to October 1990.

Competition law in the EC and in the ECSC.
See item no. 562.

Report on competition policy.
See item no. 577.

Lawyers in Europe.
See item no. 623.

Industry

General

405 **1992 and the metal and mechanical engineering sector: a report for the Europen Bureau, Department of the Taoiseach.**
T. J. Baker, S. Scott. Dublin: Stationery Office, 1989. 25p.
The endemic nature of change in the industry is stressed, with 1992 identified as only one factor among many which will affect the sector in the 1990s. The main features of the Single European Market are outlined and discussed under the headings: technical standards and regulations, public procurement, administrative barriers, frontier formalities, indirect taxes, and structural funds. Responses to the Single European Market in other countries are summarized along with other indirect effects of 1992. The conclusions drawn are that the opportunities presented by the Single Market should outweigh the dangers, mainly because of the absence of the most vulnerable type of enterprise, and because physical scale is not a dominant factor in the niche markets served by the Irish engineering sector.

406 **Getting into Europe.**
Richard Citron. London: Stoy Hayward, 1991. 445p.
This book has been written specifically for business people. It provides answers to the first three questions that management of a UK company will raise when thinking of doing business with Europe, whether exporting or investing. These are: what are the international tax implications? How will I raise finance for the new operation? How will I monitor what is going on overseas? Simple examples throughout the book help to illustrate the complex points that can arise when business spans international borders. It includes summaries of European tax systems as they apply to UK companies investing abroad, and UK executives posted overseas. There are special sections on the rules applicable to real-estate investment, and exchange control regulations in various countries and Eastern Europe. There are appendices on: European corporate tax systems, European personal tax systems, Eastern Europe, EC tax and company law harmonization, European withholding taxes. A list of useful addresses is also included.

407 **1992 and the pharmaceutical, healthcare and chemicals sector: a report for the Europen Bureau, Department of the Taoiseach.**
Coopers & Lybrand Associates. Dublin: Stationery Office, 1990. 33p.
This report on the pharmaceuticals, healthcare and chemicals sector is divided into three parts. Part I consists of a description and analysis of the sector. It includes the number of establishments and enterprises, ownership, structural analysis, volume of production, employment, productivity, investment, research, local expenditure, profits, assessment of the pharmaceuticals sector, strengths of the sector, and weaknesses of the sector. Part II lists the principal measures under the single market programme affecting the sector, directly or indirectly, or which will affect the sector, with detailed comments on the measures. Part III provides a more general assessment of the impact of the single market programme than can be obtained from a listing of measures.

408 **1992 and the construction sector: a report for the Europen Department of the Taoiseach.**
Davy Kelleher McCarthy Ltd. Dublin: Stationery Office, 1989. 81p.
Considers the various measures being implemented, as part of the process of the completion of the internal market, which will have an impact on organizations directly engaged in construction activity and on outside agencies that have a rôle in the sector. The creation of a single market for construction products, the opening up of public procurement to increased outside competition, the increase in structural fund expenditure, the harmonization of indirect taxes, the mutual recognition of higher education diplomas in respect of architects, engineers and other related professions, and other developments that will contribute to the completion of the internal market by the end of 1991, all have some implications for the construction sector and these are assessed in this study.

409 **Small and medium sized enterprises.**
Kenneth Dyson. London: Routledge, 1989. 192p.
Small firms are at the forefront of the European economy. To develop exports and fight off imports Europe's entrepreneurs have to 'think European'. This volume guides the reader through the EC's special policies for small firms.

410 **The food sector.**
Stephen Fallows. London: Routledge, 1989. 208p.
Media coverage has highlighted controversies involving the EC regulations in matters related to food law. This volume explains the rôle of EC policy in this area, and what it means for those involved in business and the public sector.

411 **1992 and the textiles, clothing and footwear sector: a report for the Europen Department of the Taoiseach.**
Fitzpatrick & Associates. Dublin: Stationery Office, 1989. 38p.
This publication, one of a series of ten on the implication of the Single European Market for key sectors of the Irish economy was written to guide industrialists through the 1992 legislation and to assist them in the formulation of strategy. Although aimed at the Irish economy, there are chapters on the pattern for the industry in the EC and on international developments.

412 **Approaches to industrial policy within the European Community and its impact on European integration.**
Fritz Franzmeyer.   Aldershot, England: Gower, 1982. 167p.
The conclusions of this study are that the Community has been no more successful in its attempts to encourage innovation and coordinate activity in new industries at the European level than in dealing with declining ones. The failure of Euratom was an early demonstration of the way in which individual countries can paralyse common policies when they believe them to be against their own interests. The Airbus project, generally regarded as a Community success, showed how disagreement can arise from commercial as well as political considerations.

413 **1992 and the tourism sector: a report for the Europen Department of the Taoiseach.**
Alan W. Gray, Yvonne Scott.   Dublin: Stationery Office, 1990. 43p.
A report on the prospects for the Irish tourist industry under the Single European Act. It is also a useful document for other member states because it gives the specific regulatory measures affecting tourism and the EC initiatives to develop tourism.

414 **Towards 1992: effects on the Scottish financial sector.**
Allan Hodgson, Ewan Brown.   Edinburgh: Single Market Committee of the Scottish Economic Council, 1989. 4p.
A useful paper because the prospect of selling financial services to a market six times the size of the UK is immensely appealing, yet the Scottish financial sector faces important challenges which will test its creative skills. In particular, the sector is hampered by a lack of capital which will constrain its ability to pursue effectively the opportunities of the Single Market. In the short term, venture capital management and the Scottish Merchant Banking sector may be the principal beneficiaries.

415 **The City and the Single European Market.**
Edited by William Kay.   Cambridge, England: Woodhead-Faulkner, 1991. 264p.
A comprehensive and up-to-date analysis of the effect of 1992 on City (i.e., financial services) businesses, this book advises on how best to anticipate and respond to the challenges and opportunities it will bring.

416 **Strategies and policies of the European Economic Community to improve the competitiveness of European industry.**
Edited by Giovanni Leodari, Antonio Mosconi.   Venice, Italy: Centre of Studies and Information, 1984. 146p.
A collection of papers delivered at a conference sponsored by the European Parliament in 1982.

417 The Single European Market and the information and communications technologies.

Edited by Gareth Locksley.   London: Belhaven, 1990. 291p.

This publication is the result of a workshop organized by researchers collaborating in the Economic and Social Research Council's Programme on Information and Communications Technologies (PICT). Their research seeks to identify and explore the factors which are influencing the development and application of advanced information and communications technologies and systems, and the implications of these technologies and systems.

418 1992 and the food and drink industry: a report for the Europen Department of the Taoiseach.

National Food Centre.   Dublin: Stationery Office, 1989. 82p.

One of a series of ten studies on the implications of the Single European Market for key sectors of the Irish economy. These studies also contain useful data for other member states, and their purpose is to guide economic operators through the confusing array of 1992 legislation and to address issues relevant to individual firms rather than produce a detailed or academic study.

419 1992 and the electronic, electrical and instrument engineering sectors: a report for the Europen Bureau, Department of the Taoiseach.

Eoin O'Malley.   Dublin: Stationery Office, 1990. 29p.

The electronic, electrical and instrument engineering sectors have been among the fastest-growing industries in Ireland in the 1980s and they now account for 18 per cent of manufacturing employment. These industries are very highly export-oriented, with over 90 per cent of their output going to export markets. The creation of the Single European Market will mean the removal of existing non-tariff barriers to trade within the European Community. These non-tariff barriers, such as discriminatory public-sector purchasing and differing technical standards and regulations, affect most branches of electronic, electrical and instrument engineering more strongly than most other industries. Consequently their removal will have a relatively significant effect on these sectors. Given the strong competition position of these industries in Ireland, the freeing of trade by the removal of non-tariff barriers should have the direct effect of creating opportunities for them which are distinctly greater than the risks involved from competing imports.

420 Industrial policies in the European Community.

Victoria Curzon Price.   London: Macmillan, for the Trade Policy Centre, 1981. 141p.

A short study of industrial policies in the Community by an advocate of negative intervention to correct imbalances.

421 The new business culture in Europe.

Peter Danton de Rouffignac.   London: Pitman, 1991. 256p.

This book looks beyond 1992 and considers the problems and challenges that business people in Europe will face during the whole decade of the 1990s.

422 **European integration: trade and industry.**
Edited by L. Alan Winters, Anthony Venables.   Cambridge, England:
Cambridge University Press, 1991. 280p.

These are studies of the likely impact of the Single European Market on trade and
industry.

423 **Access for the British electrical contracting industry to the Single
European Market.**
London: Electrical Contractors' Association, 1989. 99p.

This research report was funded jointly by the Electrical Contractors' Association and
the Department of Trade and Industry and takes the form of over 50 in-depth
interviews conducted on a face-to-face basis with well-placed individuals in the
electrical industry in all member states except Ireland. Each of the country reports is
arranged under the following headings: summary; general rules for establishing a
business; requirements for registration as an electrical contractor; requirements
relating to electrical contracting personnel; technical standards; inspection of
installations and installation designs; health and safety; contractual and commercial
matters.

424 **Europe and the new technologies.**
Brussels: Delta, 1988. 150p.

This monograph contains three reports from the Economic and Social Committee of
the European Communities. The reports contain information on current Community
programmes in the field of technological research and development, plus a brief
summary of significant research programmes initiated in Europe. There is also a review
of progress made in implementing the EEC framework programme of scientific and
technical activity for 1984–87, and an analysis of the Community proposal on a
European technological community.

425 **The European initiative: the business of television and films in the 1990s.**
London: British Screen Advisory Council, 1990. 40p.

Examines all aspects of a changing Europe for the television and film industries.

426 **Furniture focus 1992.**
Stevenage, England: Furniture Industry Research Association, 1989.
121p.

A collection of articles on the significance of 1992 and the Single European Market for
the furniture industry.

427 **The Industrial Development Board and the Single European Market.**
Belfast: Her Majesty's Stationery Office, 1990. 41p.

A useful study of what 1992 means for Northern Ireland. It analyses the threats
inherent in the Single Market environment and cogently discusses what action must be
taken.

428 **1992 a practical guide for computer services.**
London: Computer Services Association, 1990. 139p. bibliog.
The aim of this guide is to provide companies with the necessary framework and guidance to develop a Single European Market strategy based on their own current position, strengths, weaknesses and ambitions. It provides a framework with which to evaluate businesses in the light of the opportunities and threats presented by the Single European Market and also provides some suggestions of feasible strategies for different classes of computing services companies.

429 **The record industry in Europe.**
London: British Phonographic Industry, 1990. 14p.
This short pamphlet gives an excellent view of the problems faced by the record industry as a result of the Single European Act. Of the five major record companies only one is wholly British-owned, and these five companies control about 80 per cent of all sales in all mainland Europe. The problems for the industry are many but this report shows that it should find it fairly easy to adapt to change.

430 **The Scottish experience.**
Edinburgh: Single Market Committee of the Scottish Economic Council, 1990. 25p.
One of several studies by the Scottish Council that examines the likely impact of the Single Market on the economy of Scotland. It consists of eight case-studies covering industries as diverse as robotics, safety cabs, food processing, brushes and combs, and electronic weighbridges.

Patents

431 **Annual report of the European Patent Office.**
Munich: European Patent Office, 1977– . annual.
The annual reports give an insight into the procedures adopted and the success achieved within the European Patent Office (EPO). The EPO is entirely self-supporting, being financed solely by fee income from applicants.

432 **How to get a European patent: guide for applicants.**
Munich: European Patent Office, 1990. 7th ed. 80p.
The guide is intended to give firms, individual inventors and their representatives an outline of the procedure for the grant of European patents and, by giving practical hints, to smooth the way to a European patent.

433 **Protecting inventions in Europe.**
Munich: European Patent Office, 1990. 18p.
The European Patent Office (EPO) is not limited to EC countries in its dealings with patents but close co-operation between the national patent offices and the EPO has ensured the rapid success and gratifying development of the European Patent

Organization over the past ten years. The first European patent applications were filed in June 1978, and the first European patent was granted in January 1980. It was originally considered that the annual number of applications would level off at 30,000, but in 1988, after 10 years, it topped the 50,000 mark.

Social, Labour, Environmental and Educational Policy

The Social Charter

434 **Social work education and 1992.**
   Hugh Barr. London: Central Council for Education and Training in
   Social Work, 1990. 51p. (In Europe Series, no. 1).

A useful study explaining social work in Europe and the need for co-operation by
member states.

435 **European Community social policy: its impact on the UK.**
   Chris Brewster, Paul Teague. London: Institute of Personnel
   Management, 1989. 376p.

This book offers vital information to employers facing the challenges of the Single
European Market. It outlines European Community social policy and draws on
detailed research to examine the organizational, legal and administrative links between
the EC and Britain in this area. It goes beyond all previous accounts in its study of the
effect of EC policies at organization level, and it examines the possibilities for the
future development of a social Europe and its impact on the UK.

436 **The European employer: social and employment implications for
   managers on 'completing the European internal market'.**
   Richard Brown. London: British Institute of Management, 1988. 27p.

Describes proposed directives on employment protection, equal treatment, health and
safety, employee involvement, social accounts, model employment contracts, and
freedom of movement.

437 **Links and exchanges: a guide for social work education programmes.**
Crescy Cannan, Richard Colman, Karen Lyons.   London: Central
Council for Education and Training in Social Work, 1990. 20p. (In
Europe Series, no. 2).

A pamphlet giving useful information on the European Action Scheme for the
Mobility of University Students (ERASMUS) and its importance to social work
education. It includes a list of co-operative programmes between social work courses in
the UK and in other member states.

438 **The Social Charter and the Single European Market: towards a socially
responsible community.**
John Hughes, foreword by Ken Coates.   Nottingham, England:
Spokesman for European Labour Forum, 1991. 90p.

The author argues that the Community's emphasis on social dialogue and the equitable
extension of social rights need to go hand in hand with large-scale programmes of
expenditure to help disadvantaged regions, to combat discrimination against part-time
workers (reflected so starkly in women's inferior pay for work of equal value), to
tackle long-term unemployment, and to meet the needs of young people entering the
labour market. Hugh McMahon contributes a check-list on how the Social Charter is
faring from the viewpoint of the Commission's Action programme and from that of the
European Parliament.

439 **1992: the social dimension.**
F. Knox.   London: Trade and Tariffs Research, 1990. 82p.

This booklet gives the history of the EC's social dimension from the establishment of
the European Coal and Steel Community (ECSC) in the early 1950s and suggests that
emphasis on worker participation stems from circumstances peculiar to that time. It
gives details of the 1989 Social Charter and argues that there may be dangers in the
'social dumping' concept, and that the major omission of the charter is lack of
provisions against age discrimination in employment.

440 **The social dimension and cohesion: complementing or contradicting?**
Angelos Kotios, Manfred Schafers.   *Intereconomics*, vol. 25, no. 3
(May–June 1990), p. 140–6.

Whilst there is general agreement that the overall social standards of Europe have
improved, the authors of this article argue that any harmonization upward may actually
harm the free operation of the internal market. They feel that institutionally imposed
minimum standards are not necessary. The 'peripheral' states – Portugal, Spain,
Greece and Ireland – may actually be able to exploit their low labour costs to
advantage, and, if it is to be lasting, any change in their social position must be
developmental.

441 **Social Europe.**
Juliet Lodge.   *Journal of European Integration (Revue d'intégration
européenne)*, vol. 13, no. 2–3 (Winter–Spring 1990), p. 135–51.

In her own contribution to this special issue, which she edited, Juliet Lodge examines
conceptual background to 'Social Europe' and the problems it faces. Seen as a
complement to the Single European Market, the concept of 'A People's Europe' or

Social, Labour, Environmental and Educational Policy. The Social Charter

'Social Europe' is ill defined. In terms of the treaties, 'Social Europe' has a limited application, referring to the improvement of living and working conditions. In these terms it is seen not merely as an adjunct to 1992, with high employment and social well-being being key aims, but the EC does not have a treaty-based remit to redistribute wealth to achieve its aims in this area. Although the Social Charter provides an important benchmark against which to measure standards, its implementation depends on simultaneous action by all EC states, and the author suggests that a clarification and reinforcement of the overall aims of policy in this area is needed to meet the challenges of disparate policies in each member state, and, in particular, the challenges of German unification.

442   **Building a people's Europe: 1992 and the social dimension.**
Marie Maës, foreword by John Drew.   London: Whurr, 1990. 104p.

In 1992 the European Community becomes a market in which people, capital, goods and services can move freely across the national boundaries of the twelve member states. Although the primary objective of this is the creation of a single European economy, it is widely accepted that the economic, financial, fiscal and commercial elements of 1992 can be a success only if a Community programme of specific measures to provide for the welfare of the Community's inhabitants is adopted. The social dimension has therefore become an integral part of the European Community's commitment to the completion of the single market by 1992. This book offers an impartial overview of the social dimension and makes a valuable contribution to the current debate on this complex and challenging topic. As such, it will be extremely useful to those in companies or other organizations responsible for human resources, for trade union officials and representatives of trade and employee associations, and for anyone concerned with the many issues which may be affected by the social policy currently being formulated in the run-up to 1992. These issues include: health, social security, housing, the environment, the free movement of people, development funding for deprived areas, and industrial regeneration.

443   **Health care and the European Community.**
Alan Maynard.   London: Croom Helm, 1975. 284p.

A study of social welfare provisions, both public and private, for EEC countries. An impressive array of facts is presented in such a way as to give a common format for each country. There is a final chapter on comparative analysis, which is rather weak.

444   **European Community social policy: developments and issues.**
Sonia Mazey.   London: PNL Press, 1989. 28p. (European Dossier Series, 14).

A clear and concise primer on the 'social dimension'. The author follows the development of social policy since before the Treaty of Rome, and examines the place of social issues in the single market.

445   **The social charter as a counterpart to the single European market.**
Dirk Meyer.   *Intereconomics*, vol. 25, no. 6 (Nov.–Dec. 1990), p. 289–92.

This article claims that competition between social systems, which is seen as the alternative to an imposed or commonly agreed social charter, need not be harmful.

Social, Labour, Environmental and Educational Policy. The Social Charter

Local policy may indeed be more appropriate, with each member state setting its own standards, which must be related to its productivity.

446 **Mobility and social cohesion in the EC: a forward look.**
Laurie Pickup. Luxembourg: Office for Official Publications of the EC, 1990. 135p.

In an academic, but still generally relevant, study of the potential effects of worker mobility, the author surveys the impact of greater mobility, the groups affected, and the problems caused. In studying the priorities for future policy and study Pickup finds that the greatest potential impact of the single market will not be in terms of personal migration, but in terms of the mobility of other factors of production, and with them jobs and investment.

447 **Organised labour and the Social Charter.**
Robert Robinson. *European Access*, 1990, 6 (Dec. 1990), p. 12–14.

A short examination of the rôle of the European Trades Union Confederation and its part in forming the Social Charter. The author argues that the most important point for union lobbying and action is at member-state level, as it is here that the implementing measures, if any, will be taken.

448 **European social policy: today and tomorrow.**
Michael Shanks. Oxford: Pergamon, 1977. 105p.

Michael Shanks was a former Director-General of Social Affairs at the Commission and gives a clear insight into the aims and work of the Community in relation to the problems of living together. He examines the challenges posed by a combination of inflation, social deprivation and unemployment, emphasizes the need for a new mandate to strengthen the Treaty of Rome, and gives guidelines for a comprehensive programme of social reform. Job creation is an important aspect of social policy but Shanks states that 'social policy is not just about jobs, it is about life'.

449 **1992 and all that: civil liberties in the balance.**
Michael Spencer. London: Civil Liberties Trust, 1990. 184p.

What impact will 1992 and the harmonization of European Community laws have on our civil and political rights? Will refugees and third-country nationals, for example, find themselves shut out as the single Europe becomes fortress Europe? This book explains that the Social Charter, a package of measures improving employment rights and conditions (especially those of working women) along with proposals to incorporate the European convention on human rights into both Community and national law, promises potential benefits for civil liberties.

450 **Social Europe: Ariadne's thread.**
Jonathon Story. *Journal of European Integration (Revue d'intégration européenne)*, vol. 13, no. 2–3 (Winter–Spring 1990), p. 151–65.

The author examines the stances of the major parties – the Commission, Germany, France and the UK – in the EC debate on social policy, and finds the situation 'replete with paradoxes'. Despite a widespread view that European union is vital, there has been a marked reluctance to apply the logic behind this to the labour market.

However, the political dynamic may force the EC further into social issues, as the limits of what may be discussed as part of the internal market grow wider and wider, and as pressure grows from a re-unifying Germany. The author points to a basic tension between the desire for a fully mobile skilled workforce and a general desire to keep out hordes of unskilled migrants.

451 **New dimensions in European social policy.**
Edited by Jacques Vandamme, with foreword by Jacques Delors.
London: Routledge, for the Trans European Policy Studies
Association, 1985. 208p.
Considers the past evolution of European social policy and the issues affecting it over the next decade.

452 **Health and safety at work in the EC.**
Social Europe, 2/90, 1990. 242p.
Aimed at any audience with a need to know about health and safety issues, such as employers, lobby groups or trade unions. This issue presents a series of articles on the questions involved in an EC health and safety policy, and usefully includes the full texts of current Community legislation in this field. Articles by EC officials and representatives from both sides of industry cover the inputs to policy-making, the rôle of health and safety in the Single Market, national policy and legislation, and safety issues in extractive industries. Texts are provided not only of current legislation, but of other key Commission documents, e.g., the schedule of occupational diseases.

453 **1992 – the social dimension.**
Luxembourg: Office of Official Publications of the EC, 1990. 87p.
(*European Documentation*, 2/1990).
This official publication gives the European Communities' own view of the need for a social and labour dimension to the internal market – 'the internal market . . . will first and foremost have to serve the citizens of the European Community'. This is a straightforward and accessible introduction to the major areas of employee mobility and protection, health and safety, the Social Charter, and the measures needed to create a European 'social area'.

454 **Workers' rights and 1992.**
London: Labour Research Department, 1990. 40p.
A booklet explaining the implications for workers of the European social charter and the action programme.

Comparative tables of the social security schemes in the member states of the European Communities.
See item no. 559.

Compendium of Community provisions on social security.
See item no. 561.

Labour and the trade unions

455 The European labour movement and European integration.
Barbara Barnouin. London: Pinter, 1986. 200p. bibliog.

A study of international relationships between non-government organizations with particular reference to the case of national trade union bodies in Western Europe. The author investigates the response of trade unions since 1945 to the increasingly complex manufacturing relationships and dependencies between European countries, in particular in the light of the establishment of the European Economic Community. Of particular interest is the chapter explaining the objectives and organizational structure of the European Trades Union Confederation.

456 A trade union strategy in the Common Market.
Edited by Ken Coates. Nottingham, England: Spokesman Books, 1971. 149p.

This is a translation of the report on workers' control by the Fédération Générale du Travail de Belgique (Belgian General Federation of Labour), together with supporting documents.

457 The Labour movement in Europe.
Walter Kendall. London: Allen & Unwin, 1975. 456p.

Europe in this context means the countries which are members of the EEC. Kendall shows how the Labour movement has developed in each country and no two countries are alike. They differ according to the time of arrival of the industrial revolution, the attitude of the Church, the state of national unity, or the power of the monarchy. There is a chapter on international trade unionism and the final chapter looks into the future.

458 Trade unions as a pressure group in the European Community.
Emil Joseph Kirchner. Farnborough, England: Saxon House, 1977. 208p.

This is a study of action taken by trade unions in lobbying the EEC, particularly the Commission, on such matters as the harmonization of vocational training, social security in general, and the development of the European Social Fund. It also deals with the work of pressure groups for social security benefits for social workers.

459 Management and labour in Europe: the industrial enterprise in Germany, Britain and France.
Christel Lane. Aldershot, England: Edward Elgar, 1989. 344p.

This clear, logical and helpful book systematically compares the structural and behavioural aspects of business organization in Britain with their equivalents in more economically successful European societies, France and Germany.

460 **What price Europe?**
Jack Peel, foreword by Baroness Elles.   Fleet, England: Common
Cause Publications, 1990. 63p.

Jack Peel was director of industrial relations at the European Commission in Brussels
from 1973 to 1981. He gained a unique insight into the various ways member countries
of the Community approach these and many other questions. From his first-hand
experience the author examines various practical aspects of British and European
Community industrial relations and assesses their future direction. An introductory
chapter describes contemporary theories on what makes people want to work and goes
on to examine the ways in which different countries, ranging from the USA and Japan
to Scandinavian and Western European states, approach the questions of motivation,
incentive, and industrial relations.

461 **Free movement of labour in the Single European Market.**
Heinz Werner.   *Intereconomics*, vol. 25, no. 2 (March–April 1990),
p. 77–81.

In this article the author examines the possible effects of '1992' on labour mobility both
in theoretical terms and in practice. He argues that an overall increase in economic
activity may mean that previous areas of net labour supply, such as Portugal, will
experience greater domestic demand. However, only a small percentage of the EC's
workforce will be actively mobile, since only a small number of people will meet the
necessary requirements of language skills and qualifications.

462 **Europe 1992: progress report on trade union objectives.**
London: Trades Union Congress, 1989. 43p.

A clearly written report on the progress and aims of the TUC towards the Single
European Act. It deals with influencing the legislative programme, the Social Charter,
the Delors Committee report and trade union response in the UK.

463 **Maximising the benefits: minimising the costs.**
London: Trades Union Congress, 1989. 30p.

Outlines issue by issue the UK TUC's thinking on the labour–management and trade
union issues raised by the Internal Market, and the needs of what is seen as an
increasingly mobile workforce. There is some brief discussion of such topics as worker
participation, information flows and training needs.

Trade union information bulletin.
See item no. 627.

Unemployment

464 **Corporate employment policies for the Single European Market.**
John Atkinson.   London: Institute of Manpower Studies, 1989. 107p.

This report shows how far employers are already moving towards a single European
labour market. Pressure for international integration comes from the EC harmoniza-

tion process itself, from a tendency in multinationals to organize in business streams across national borders, and from a concern about current and prospective skill shortages leading to a widening of recruitment nets. Despite this pressure to internationalize their business operations, the report shows that respondents staffed the bulk of their workforces within national labour markets. But employers were developing an internationally mobile cadre among four small but vital groups of employees, namely, senior managers; leading scientific and technical personnel; future senior managers earmarked for management development; and new graduates.

465 **Europe's unemployment problem.**
Edited by Jacques H. Dreze, Charles R. Bean. London: M.I.T. Press, 1991. 504p.
A joint effort by researchers in ten countries, presenting the findings of the European Unemployment Programme. It gives the causes of unemployment in Europe since 1975, and suggests remedies.

466 **Combating long-term unemployment: local/EEC relations.**
Kenneth Dyson. London: Routledge, 1989. 224p.
This title represents the first attempts to analyse local–EEC relations in politics towards long-term unemployment. It offers examples of comparative analysis of particular aspects of these policies.

Personnel management

467 **Industrial relations in the Common Market.**
Campbell Balfour. London; Boston: Routledge & Kegan Paul, 1972. 132p.
Balfour argues that joining the EEC will not solve Britain's economic malaise, particularly with regard to labour relations. It gives the state of play in 1971 but admits that there is no common norm of industrial relations.

468 **European management guides.**
Incomes Data Services. London: Institute of Personnel Management, 1990–92. 5 vols.
The Institute of Personnel Management commissioned Incomes Data Services to report on all aspects of employment practice throughout the EC member states. The result of this research is published in 5 volumes which contain an outline of existing and proposed EC legislation, detailed country-by-country analysis with practical information and guidance on how the subject is approached, references back to UK practice and law to illustrate similarities and differences, and clear pointers to further sources of more detailed information. The five volumes (all of 150 pages) are:
Recruitment, 1990. After discussing the labour market this volume deals with the custom, practice and law on recruitment procedures, how to find the applicants, recruitment documents, making the choice, and the law and practices of handling rejection of unsuccessful candidates.

Social, Labour, Environmental and Educational Policy. Personnel management

Terms and conditions of appointment, 1990. This volume deals with constitutional and statutory rights of employees, contracts of employment, basic conditions, individual workplace rights, equal treatment, work environment and termination of employment.

Industrial relations, 1991. There are chapters on statutory and agreed mechanisms for employee participation, trade union law, law on industrial act and voluntary conciliation machinery.

Pay and benefits, 1991. Collective bargaining and the rôle and influence of government, unions and employers' organizations are explained, as is also pay determination for employees not covered by collective bargaining. Non-basic pay, equal pay, merit pay are dealt with and there is an appendix on labour costs.

Training and development, 1992. Educational systems are explained, as are occupational training schemes, tertiary education and qualifications. There are details of company policies and collective regulation of training and also about management education and development.

469 **1992: personnel management and the single European market.**

Incomes Data Services and the Institute of Personnel Management.

London: Institute of Personnel Management, 1988. 60p.

This publication, researched and produced by Incomes Data Services in association with the Institute of Personnel Management, will help UK managers devise policies and practices that will be acceptable in a continent where national rules, practices and management cultures vary considerably.

470 **Employment policy.**

Margareta Holmstedt. London: Routledge, 1991. 176p.

With new working patterns, flexible working practices, new employment rights and a legal framework to implement within the EC, this guide is a reference work for everyone from trade unions to employers.

471 **Personnel management for the Single European Market.**

Mark Pinder. London: Pitman, 1990. 267p.

Part one of this book takes a global view of the Single European Market, examining its origins and the objectives; Part two examines the challenges faced by the personnel manager; Part three attempts to answer how these challenges can be met; and Part four links the first three parts by the use of case-studies.

472 **EC labour market policy.**

Paul Teague, John Grahl. *Journal of European Integration (Revue d'intégration européenne)*, vol. 13, no. 1 (Fall 1989), p. 55–73.

The authors argue that, regardless of any direction of official policy, the Community's involvement in labour market issues will increase, because market integration and other measures are producing changes to equal opportunities legislation and to laws regarding health and safety, and because changes to the structure of the EC judicial process will mean that more citizens have recourse to it. Examining the conflicting views of labour market policy – broadly, interventionist versus laissez-faire – they conclude that the formation of social/labour policy will represent an acid test for the 'new age' in EC policy-making.

Sex equality

473 **Women, equality and Europe.**
Edited by M. Buckley, M. Anderson. London: Macmillan, 1988.
228p.

A collection of essays giving a clear assessment of what effect the EC equality laws will have on women. Some of the best essays are on the employment of part-time women workers (there are about 3,000,000 in the UK alone) and the way loopholes are found to avoid the law.

474 **Women's rights and the EEC: a guide for women in the UK.**
Vanessa Hall-Smith, Catherine Hoskyns, Judy Keiner, Erika
Szyszczak. London: Rights of Women Europe, 1983. 161p.

Rights of Women is a collective of feminine legal workers which aims to understand the practical and ideological effects of the law and legal services on women's lives, with a view to making them more responsive to women's needs and interests. This publication includes explanations about getting money for 'women only' training projects and fighting discrimination in employment and education; it challenges unfair social security rules for women and gives details of the struggle against racist immigration rules.

475 **Sex equality policies in the European Community.**
Elizabeth Meehan. *Journal of European Integration (Revue d'intégration européenne)*, vol. 13, no. 2–3 (Winter–Spring 1990), p. 184–96.

An examination of Community policy and Court of Justice decisions advancing the cause of sexual equality. The author argues that the Social Charter, although a potent symbol for women, has failed to tackle the basic issues behind sex-based discrimination. However, both the Commission and the European Parliament need popular support, and need to be seen to be trying to offset the negative employment effects of the Single Market, and this means that women may reasonably expect real improvements in their position.

476 **The 1990's: the decade for women in Europe.**
London: European Parliamentary Labour Party, 1990. 12p.

A slim pamphlet written by the Women's Rights Committee in the European Parliament. It sets out their campaign to develop genuine equality between women and men.

Women of Europe.
See item no. 583.

Environmental policy

477 EEC environmental policy and Britain.
Nigel Haigh.   Harlow, England: Longman, 1990. 2nd rev. ed. 382p.

This handbook is a guide to environmental legislation, including all relevant directives, regulations and decisions. It gives essential, current data on water, waste, air, chemicals, wildlife and countryside, and noise and environmental impact assessment. Over 200 items of EEC legislation are covered and clearly summarized. British legislation is also closely examined. The second revised edition has been up-dated to 1990 and includes a postscript on the Environment Protection Bill and its implications. There is also the *European environmental yearbook* by the Institute for Environmental Studies (Milan; London: DocTer International, 1991. 2nd ed. 1100p.) which presents an up-to-date summary of information on nature conservancy and town and country planning in the twelve member states of the European Communities. The *Yearbook* falls into four sections. The first deals, in encyclopaedic form, with the twenty-two main topics listed in alphabetical order; these include agriculture and environment, energy and nuclear safety, financing the environment, pollution, sea/coasts – protection and management, toxic and hazardous substances, water supply and river management. The object of this compendium is to provide readers with a comparative study of the institutional picture, administration and departmental resources, and policies pursued by individual member states in the various areas concerned. The section closes with a bibliography. The second section contains four special environmental surveys which explain the influence on Europe and vice versa, of measures taken in Australia, Japan, the USA and the USSR. The third section of the *Yearbook* lists the legislation adopted in the EC countries and EC directives on the environment, as well as the most significant international agreements on the subject, indicating their degree of implementation. It also contains international conventions. The final section is concerned with documentation, protocols, EC programmes and Acts.

478 The environment policy of the European Communities.
Stanley P. Johnson, Guy Corcelle, preface by Jacques Delors.
London: Graham & Trotman, 1989. 210p.

This book provides a complete survey of the extensive legislation on environmental policy introduced by the European Communities.

479 Greening the Treaty: strengthening environmental policy in the Treaty of Rome.
David Wilkinson.   London: Institute for European Environmental Policy, 1990. 27p.

A review of amendments on environmental matters put forward for discussion by the Intergovernmental Conference convened by the Italian government in December 1990.

480 Ten years of Community environment policy.
Luxembourg: Office for Official Publications of the European Communities, 1984. 104p.

A decade of slow progress in environmental matters is examined, and a very clear explanation of the aims and principles of the EC environment policy is given.

State of the environment.
See item no. 593.

European Environment.
See item no. 617.

Education

481 **Youth policy.**
Gordon Blakely. London: Routledge, 1990. 192p.
With a shrinking workforce, training young people is vital. The EC has a crucial role to play in the economic, social, educational and cultural development of the population. This study examines the alternatives.

482 **Britain and a single market Europe: prospects for a common school curriculum.**
Martin McLean. London: Kogan Page, in association with the Institute of Education, University of London, 1990. 148p.
'1992' will have profound implications for education and this book examines the economic and social pressures for curriculum harmonization across Europe, studies the variants in curriculum philosophies in major European countries, and looks at the implications for England and Wales.

483 **The EEC and education.**
Guy Neave. Stoke-on-Trent, England: Trentham Books, for the European Institute of Education and Social Policy, 1984. 203p.
An overview of what has been undertaken and what needs to be achieved by the EC in the field of education.

484 **Higher education in Scotland and the European Community.**
William A. Turmeau, Malcolm C. MacLennan. Glasgow: Industry Department of Scotland, for the Single Market Committee of the Scottish Economic Council, 1990. 20p.
This paper is intended to highlight the rôle of higher education in the period leading up to the achievement of the Single European Market in 1992 – and indeed beyond. In particular, the paper attempts to evaluate the part which higher education can play in co-operation and association with industry and commerce in ensuring that Scotland takes maximum advantage of the Single European Market. The great importance of education to the European Community is described and the importance of higher education in particular is emphasized. Current co-operation initiatives and incentives are detailed and information is provided on various European schemes designed to promote co-operation within and between higher education and industry and commerce. Future policy, programmes and initiatives being put forward by the European Community are detailed.

485 **Higher education in the European Community.**
London: Kogan Page, for the European Communities, 1985. 300p.
The bulk of this student handbook is made up of similarly structured accounts for each member state. The headings used are: organization of higher education, admission and registration, knowledge of the language of instruction, financial assistance and scholarships, entry and residence regulations, social aspects (social security and health insurance; advisory services; student employment; student organizations; cost of living; accommodation; services for students; facilities for disabled students), sources of information, appendices (addresses; bibliography; survey of courses of study at higher education institutions; glossary). In addition it also contains information about the European University Institute in Florence, the College of Europe in Bruges, grants from the EC for the development of joint study programmes, information centres for the academic recognition of diplomas and of periods of study in the European Community.

486 **Scottish perspectives on foreign language skills.**
Single Market Committee of the Scottish Economic Council.
Edinburgh: Scottish Office, 1991. 8p.
The Single Market Committee of the Scottish Economic Council was established by the Secretary of State for Scotland in 1988. Its remit is to examine the likely impact of the Single Market on the economy of Scotland, and to submit proposals designed to encourage those concerned in both public and private sectors to prepare for it. The Committee has discussed and examined the important issue of foreign-language training and decided to publish this paper in the hope that it will encourage more Scottish companies, particularly small and medium-sized firms, to take steps to improve the linguistic capabilities within their businesses.

Directory of higher education institutions.
See item no. 565.

ERASMUS Newsletter.
See item no. 566.

European University News.
See item no. 571.

Transport Policy

General

487 Transport and European integration.
Carlo degli Abbati. Luxembourg: Office for Official Publications of
the European Communities, 1987. 229p. (European Perspectives, 15).
Although sponsored and published by the EC this publication is by no means an
uncritical look at EC policy. It is an academic and highly detailed study of all aspects of
transport in Europe, including market organization, policy development and
background. The study concludes that there has been a 'conspicuous failure to achieve
the basic objective of a common transport policy'. Although much has been achieved,
many measures have been held up, mainly because of intransigence – some French, but
particularly British. And behind the political dimension there are other problems; for
example, a lack of real progress in transportation systems since the 1930s. The study
suggests that institutional change in the EC is needed, with a more powerful
parliament, and a possible sanctioning of a 'two speed Europe.'

488 Air transport and the EEC.
John Balfour. *European Access*, 1990, 2 (April), p. 13–15.
Very slow progress has been made in creating an internal market for air transport and
it is unlikely that it will be fully completed by 1992. This article explains the progress
which has been made and which is accelerating.

489 Flying high: airline prices and European regulations.
Sean D. Barrett. Aldershot, England: Gower, for the Adam Smith
Institute, 1988. 96p.
The author compares European air fares with those over similar distances in the
United States, and argues that the experience of deregulation in the United States
'strongly supports the introduction of low cost carriers in Europe'. He goes on to argue
that 'liberalizing the regulation of international aviation requires innovative thinking

and action by governments and regulators, by the currently protected airlines in order
to face competition, by airport authorities to minimize their costs and in the retailing of
airline tickets'. There is a dearth of serious writing on a common transport policy and
this pamphlet is a welcome contribution to the argument on establishing free trade in
the service sector generally. This is a one-sided view and argues (as one would expect
from the Adam Smith Institute) for a free market.

490 **Road haulage licensing and EC transport policy.**
     K. J. Button.   Aldershot, England: Gower, 1984. 127p.
There are relatively few books on EC transport policy and this monograph goes some
way to fill a gap. The excellent references allow for follow-up research.

491 **External relations in the air transport section: air transport policy or the
     Common Commercial Policy?**
     G. Close.   *Common Market Law Review*, vol. 27, no. 1 (Spring 1990),
     p. 107–27.
A legal study of EC air transport policy and its link with overall commercial policy,
examining Commission statements and case law. The author examines the rights of
member states to conclude bi-lateral agreements in this sector and demonstrates how
the issues involved can have wider ramifications for the nature of the EC.

492 **1992 and the transport sector: a report for the Europen [sic] Bureau
     Department of the Taoiseach.**
     James Crowley.   Dublin: Stationery Office, 1990. 62p.
Ireland's successful participation in the Single Market will depend in part on the extent
to which the handicaps presented by the country's peripheral location, island status,
small size, need to import raw materials, and the generally poor quality of its internal
transport network, can be overcome. The purpose of the report is to assess the impact
of the EC Single Market on Ireland's transport sector, and the transport needs of the
Irish economy in the trading environment which the Single Market will create.

493 **The transport policy of the European Community.**
     Nigel Despicht.   London: PEP and Chatham House, 1970. 85p.
Despicht gives explanations of the slow progress that the Community had made on
transport policy, believing that the Commission showed excessive zeal in trying to
establish a transport policy on too grand a scale. National transport policies and the
Treaty of Rome's provisions are clearly explained.

494 **The European Community transport policy: towards a common
     transport policy.**
     Jürgen Erdmenger.   Aldershot, England: Gower, 1984. 155p.
The Treaty of Rome states the need for a common transport policy and also mentions
certain issues such as the rules to govern transport between members and the
application of the rules of establishment, competition and the like. The integration of
the market both requires, and is dependent upon, simple, free passage of both goods
and people and the growing volume of intra-Community trade makes this increasingly
obvious. Increased traffic flows create more congestion, more environmental stress and
require more investment. New members have meant the geographical extension of the

market and brought new interests in shipping. Non-members are also affected, for much Community traffic passes across Switzerland and Austria on its north–south route, whilst Yugoslavia has become a transit path between Greece and her Community partners. But the author states that a Common Transport Policy will not become a reality without the political will to achieve this objective.

495 Transport law of the European Community.
Rosa Greaves.   London: Athlone Press, 1991. 240p.

Writing on EC transport policy is limited so this is a useful study of the impact of community transport law on member states.

496 Transport policy.
Kerry Hamilton.   London: Routledge, 1990. 160p.

Although the Channel Tunnel is the most talked-about development, the EC is actively supporting improvements in the transport infrastructure. This publication gives an overview of what progress, even if slow, has been made.

497 European aviation: a common market?
Francis McGowan, Chris Trengrove.   London: Institute of Fiscal Studies, 1986. 156p. (Report no. 23).

This study sets out to show just how high the price of European air transport is and assesses whether the current EEC proposals will succeed in increasing competition and bringing down fares. It also examines alternative paths to reform, notably the UK Government's policy of liberalizing air services.

498 Improving Britain's links with Europe.
Derek Palmer.   *National Westminster Bank Quarterly Review* (Aug. 1989), p. 29–38.

The author points up inadequacies in European, and particularly British, transport infrastructure in the light of the possible demands of the internal market. He claims that without improvements peripheral regions will fail to benefit to the same extent as the centre.

499 Transport policy in the EEC.
John Whitelegs.   London: Routledge & Kegan Paul, 1989. 256p.

Transport policy is largely determined by member states but the crux of the successful conclusion of the internal market is to complete the common transport policy. This book deals briefly with most aspects of transport as it is, but in assessing an area where rapid change is expected, much could become dated. However, the main issues remain and these are well documented.

500 Changing the skylines.
Management Today (Jan. 1989), p. 93–101.

Examines the problems relating to airline deregulation, competition, co-operation and airport capacity in Europe, in the light of US experience since 1978.

501 **European Community transport policy in the approach to 1992.**
European File, 9/90 (Aug. 1990). 11p.

The EC's basic introduction to transport and the single market. It is intended as an introduction and primer only, and those needing detailed or scholarly treatment should look elsewhere. That said, this is clear, straightforward and well presented, and is a good starting point for further work.

Europa Transport: Observation of the transport markets.
See item no. 568.

The Channel Tunnel

502 **Approaching the Channel Tunnel.**
Edited by Clive Church. Canterbury, England: University Association for Contemporary European Studies, 1988. 76p. (UACES Occasional Papers, no. 3).

These printed papers from an academic colloquium about the tunnel include views of the tunnel from both France and the UK. Essays discuss the financial and legal aspects of the project, planning and environmental considerations, and the place of the tunnel in transport integration. The conclusion is that the real questions raised by the tunnel are not those of viability, but of its impact, control over it, and its benefits. A full working through of the attitudes and questions raised by the project can play an important rôle in the future of EC integration.

503 **The Tunnel: the Channel and beyond.**
Edited by Bronwen Jones. Chichester, England: Ellis Horwood, 1987. 334p.

Suitable for both a specialist and a general audience, this collection of essays covers the background politics, finance and history of the Channel Tunnel, together with examinations of its economic, environmental and employment impacts. The technology and future prospects of the tunnel are also covered, and the essays present a variety of viewpoints.

504 **The Channel Tunnel.**
Institution of Civil Engineers. London: Thomas Telford, 1989. 331p.

A collection of papers from an Institution of Civil Engineers conference, presenting detailed discussion of many aspects of the tunnel project – its history and political background, its management and design, and the place of the tunnel in transport in Europe. Some of the papers in this volume are highly technical, but the more general papers are stimulating and readily accessible, offering valuable insights.

Energy Policy

505   **National versus supra-national interests and the problem of establishing an effective EC energy policy.**
Ali M. El Agraa, Yao-Su Hu.   *Journal of Common Market Studies*, vol. 22, no. 4 (June 1984), p. 333–50.

A systematic academic evaluation of the development of an EC energy policy, which begins with the need for a policy, and ends by observing that the issues involved in trans-frontier energy planning mean that energy policy is very closely bound in with overall integration. Detailed treatment is given to coal and nuclear energy policies, and the authors suggest that the EC lacks both a clear vision of the future and clear policy tools in this area.

506   **Energy in the European countries.**
Edited by Frans A. M. Alting von Geusau.   Leyden, The Netherlands: Sijthoff, 1975. 213p.

A not very well edited series of papers given at a meeting on energy policy planning in May 1974 at the John F. Kennedy Institute of Tilburg. There are, however, interesting and informative papers on nuclear power. The papers on oil and gas are controversial but are not labelled as such.

507   **Energy and the environment: striking a balance?**
Leigh Hancher.   *Common Market Law Review*, vol. 26, no. 3 (1989), p. 475–512.

An examination of the possibility of a more co-ordinated approach to fuel supply, energy provision and environmental concerns. The author argues that although the Single European Act gives the Community potential legal tools in this area these are not sufficient to enable it to overcome the resistance of member states to a co-ordinated strategy on environmental protection.

119

508 **A single market for oil and gas: the legal obstacles.**
Leigh Hancher. *Journal of Energy and Natural Resources Law*, vol. 8,
no. 2 (1990), p. 77–104.

The author examines the place of oil and gas in the Commission's strategic thinking,
and the importance of these resources for the Community. The structure of each
industry is discussed, together with the legal basis for Commission action and the
problems posed by the nature of the industries for the application of EC competition
law.

509 **Electricity in Europe: opening the market.**
Andrew Holmes.   London: Financial Times, 1988. 2nd ed. 131p.

This report analyses the major issues facing Europe's electricity industry, and forecasts
the changes expected in the 1990s. It describes in detail the structure, policies and
performance of the electricity supply companies in Western and Eastern Europe, with
comprehensive statistical information presented in a format allowing inter-country
comparisons to be readily made.

510 **Energy and the European Community.**
N. J. D. Lucas.   London: Europa, for the David Davies Memorial
Institute of International Studies, 1977. 175p.

A well-written analysis of the historical evolution of European energy policy up to
1973.

511 **The single energy market and energy policy: conflicting agendas?**
Francis McGowan.   *Energy Policy*, vol. 17, no. 6 (Dec. 1989),
p. 547–53.

McGowan examines the conflict between the traditional need for a buffer against
'energy shocks' and the opening up of the energy market to market forces as
necessitated by the completion of the internal market. The two viewpoints on energy
policy are examined against the background of attempts in the 1980s to create a
Common Energy Policy.

512 **Towards a European electricity market.**
Francis McGowan.   *World Today*, vol. 46, no. 1 (Jan. 1990), p. 15–19.

An examination of the tensions between the need to integrate electricity into the
internal market and pressures for continued national control in this area. The author
examines the possible effects of the Single Market on the structure of the industry, and
concludes that it is doubtful if governments can give up their own control over their
power supplies.

513 **Europe and world energy.**
Hanns Maull.   London: Butterworth, in association with the Sussex
European Research Centre, University of Sussex, 1980. 342p.

A wide-ranging study of Western Europe's present and future energy requirements. It
concludes by suggesting possible solutions to the problem of long-term security of
supply.

514 **Energy for a new century.**
Energy in Europe, Special Issue, July 1990. 257p.

A major report on energy issues in Europe, together with proceedings from a 1990 Commission-hosted conference, presenting important contributions from a variety of viewpoints. Coverage includes geopolitics, environmental issues, and the links between energy issues and economic growth. There is a detailed and extensive statistical and technical annexe.

515 **Energy in the European Community.**
European Documentation, 7/1990. 46p.

This is the Community's own general introduction to energy questions in Europe. It is clear and accessible, but never over-simplistic. The booklet outlines the crucial rôle of energy in the European economy, Europe's reactions to the 'oil shock', and examines EC policy objectives and the mechanism for their realization.

516 **The internal energy market.**
Energy in Europe, Special Issue, 1988. 59p.

This special issue examines the problems which may be encountered in incorporating energy into the single market. Three related problems are highlighted: the product itself is not homogeneous; the participants in the market are very diverse; and end-use of energy products is very varied. Despite these problems energy must be incorporated in the internal market if costs are to be reduced. The paper goes on to examine the legislative measures needed to incorporate energy into the single market, the nature of the energy industry, intra-EC trade in energy, energy imports and the impact of technology, and suggests possible lines for future EC action.

517 **A single European market in energy.**
London: Royal Institute of International Affairs, 1989. 40p.

There are immense institutional barriers against competition, both nationally and community-wide, which act as real constraints on the achievement of a single market in energy. This study examines the problems in each of the fuel sectors, as well as the cross-cutting issues of environment, supply security, taxation, and infrastructural integration.

Energy in Europe.
See item no. 587.

Economic, Financial and Fiscal Affairs

General

518   **Finance from the European Communities.**
Carol Cosgrove.   London: CKL Europe, 1991. 32p.
This pamphlet is a comprehensive directory of all the important development funds in
Europe. In addition, it gives much other basic information on the European
Communities.

519   **Banking in the EEC: structures and sources of finance.**
Anne Hendrie.   London: Financial Times Business Information, 1988.
370p.
In this publication the operation, supervision and regulation of each national financial
system is explained, together with the laws governing the establishing of new financial
businesses. Each country chapter has been contributed by a banking expert, and covers
the banking system, with a summary of banking legislation, the central bank, banking
supervision and regulation, banking and other financial institutions, capital and money
markets, up-to-date statistics, and a directory of banks (addresses, telephone/telex
numbers). Appendices cover business organization, taxation and exchange controls.

520   **Capital markets in the EEC: the sources and uses of medium- and long-
term finance.**
E. Victor Morgan, Richard Harrington.   London: Wilton House,
1977. 496p.
This 'Wilton House Special Study' describes the main features of the EEC capital
markets. It also has analytical chapters dealing with the supply and relative cost of
capital for industry, housing, for small firms, for the public sector and for multinational
companies.

521 **The new Europe: economic developments towards 2000.**
London: Euromonitor, 1990. 178p.
What is the future pattern of investment and trade in the new Europe? Where do the growth prospects for European business lie? This report attempts to find the answers.

Monetary System and Union

522 **Strategies for monetary integration re-visited.**
D. Cobham. *Journal of Common Market Studies*, vol. 28, no. 3 (March 1989), p. 203–18.
The author reviews the debate on integration strategy in the 1970s and evaluates the European Monetary System (EMS) in the light of this debate. He finds it to be a successful strategy for co-ordination, but notes that tensions remain between co-ordination and centralization. Cobham suggests that a possible way around this problem may be to win public opinion away from the symbolism of national sovereignty.

523 **Prospects for the European Monetary System.**
Edited by Piero Ferri. London: Macmillan, 1990. 260p.
A useful collection of conference papers on the European Monetary System (EMS). What makes it particularly valuable is that it concentrates solely on the EMS and not on plans for a wider monetary union.

524 **The European Monetary System.**
Edited by Francesco Giavazzi, Stefano Micossi, Marcus Miller.
Cambridge, England: Cambridge University Press, 1989. 448p.
This volume is the result of a conference held in Perugia in October 1987 and sponsored by the Banca d'Italia, the Centro Interuniversitario di Studi Teorici per la Politica Economica and the Centre for Economic Policy Research. Contributions include: a long-term view of the European Monetary System (EMS) by Tommaso Padoa-Schioppa; a discussion of the international environment facing the EMS by Rudiger Dornbusch; four papers under the heading 'Disinflation, external adjustment and cooperation' by Jacques Melitz, Francesco Giavazzi and Alberto Gionvannini, Susan Collins, and Stefano Vona and Lorenzo Bina Smaghi; and five papers under the heading 'Exchange rates, capital mobility and monetary coordination' by Michael Artis and Mark Taylor, John Drifill, Maurise Obstfeld, Massimo Russo and Giuseppe Tullio, and Cristina Mastropasqua, Stefano Micossi and Roberto Rinaldi. The papers offer a summary of current research, while the concluding panel discussion provides a valuable perspective on the concerns of policy-makers. A basic reference for anyone interested in the international monetary system and policy co-ordination.

Economic, Financial and Fiscal Affairs. Monetary System and Union

525   **The ECU and European monetary integration.**
Edited by Paul de Grauwe, Theo Peeters.   London: Macmillan, for
the Catholic University of Leuven, 1989. 222p.

This publication arises from a conference held at Leuven in June 1987. It includes
papers by David Lomax and Alfonso Jozzo on the use of the European Currency Unit
(ECU) as an investment currency and for invoicing purposes; a historical-comparative
paper by Michael Bordo and Anna Schwartz; papers by Polly Reynolds Allen and
Alfred Steinherr analysing the contribution of the ECU to European monetary
management and integration; a paper by Thygesen which draws on the history of the
US Federal Reserve System to make proposals for a half-way house in Europe
between the EMS and full monetary union; and a panel discussion on the ECU and the
international monetary system.

526   **Financial integration in Western Europe.**
Etienne-Sadi Kirschen, with the collaboration of Henry Simon Bloch,
William Bruce Bassett, foreword by Andrew W. Cordier.   New York:
Columbia University Press, 1969. 144p.

This early monograph on the financial integration of the Common Market deals with
the difficulties faced by the European Economic Community, when it had only six
members, in reconciling national policies, liberalizing the flow of capital, and
restructuring (if not creating new) institutions in the fields of money, banking and
security exchanges. An English translation of 'The main articles of the Rome Treaty
(of 1957) concerning the establishment of the Common Market' is appended.

527   **Monetary integration in western Europe: EMU, EMS and beyond.**
D. C. Kruse.   London; Boston: Butterworth, 1980. 274p.

This study, which starts from the Barre report and the Hague summit of 1969 when the
European Monetary Union (EMU) was launched, covers its difficult progress and the
launch of the European Monetary System (EMS). The author feels that as long as
economic objectives are set by member states on the basis of national interest only
very little progress can be made.

528   **Fiscal harmonisation: an analysis of the European Commission's
proposals.**
Catherine Lee, Mark Pearson, Stephen Smith.   London: Institute of
Fiscal Studies, 1988. 64p. (Report no. 28).

Proposals being considered by the European Community would involve far-reaching
changes to indirect taxation in EEC member states. In the UK, the proposals could
mean that value-added tax (VAT) would be imposed on a range of goods, including
food, books and children's clothing, which are not at present subject to VAT. The
Commission is also proposing major changes to the excise duties on alcohol, tobacco
and mineral oils. This report analyses the background to the Commission's proposals,
including the relationship between fiscal harmonization and the EEC objective of a
single, frontier-free internal market. It discusses the reasons why a European
Community clearing-house for VAT has been proposed, and the implications of
abolishing fiscal checks at frontiers for excise duties on alcohol, petrol and tobacco. It
includes calculations of what the proposals imply for the public finances of member
states, and what the distributional effects would be of the proposed extension of VAT
to food and other zero-rated goods. The report identifies which aspects of the

Commission's fiscal harmonization proposals are essential to the creation of a frontier-free internal market, and which are not. It concludes with some suggestions of how the Commission's proposals coud be modified to allow the internal market programme to proceed, whilst avoiding some of the more contentious fiscal changes.

529 **The making of the European Monetary System: a case study of the politics of the European Community.**
Peter Ludlow.   London: Butterworth, 1982. 319p.
The aim of this book is to analyse the origins of the European Monetary System (EMS). It is more concerned with the political implications than with the technical details.

530 **The EMS towards 1992 and beyond.**
F. McDonald, George Zis.   *Journal of Common Market Studies*, vol. 27, no. 3 (March 1989), p. 183–202.
The authors review the achievements of the European Monetary System: they point to lower inflation rates, reduced volatility in exchange rates and a reduction in money supply growth. They paint a picture of a system well provided with the mechanisms for its future survival, but they conclude that unless economic and monetary union becomes a reality the system will be threatened by the Single Market.

531 **European monetary unification.**
Giovanni Magnifico, foreword by Guido Carli.   London: Macmillan, 1973. 227p.
Magnifico, a former head of Banca d'Italia in Frankfurt and London before returning to Rome as head of the bank's department of international economic co-operation, is an advocate of a European Bank which would issue and manage a new currency, then called the *Europa*, now the *écu*. This currency would circulate with national currencies. He states that 'monetary unification should be pursued with the primary object of solving the internal problems of growth and balance within the participating countries and regions'. He lays great emphasis on regions. Non-specialists will find this volume helpful and readable.

532 **The case for a new ECU: towards another monetary system.**
Jacques Riboud, translated by Stephen Harrison.   London: Macmillan, 1989. 209p.
About 50 per cent of this book is devoted to setting out a basic theory of money and monetary policy, and to developing an argument for a new kind of European Currency Unit (ECU).

533 **The stable external currency for Europe.**
Jacques Riboud, translated by Stephen Harrison, with a foreword by Sir Alan Walters.   London: Macmillan, 1990. 190p.
The author does not believe that the governments of the European Community, even supposing that they can agree on the matter, will succeed in imposing the ECU as a payment and reserve currency for use in the EEC's external trade. In the external market the choice of currency is free and a brand new currency will be chosen only if it is better than all the alternatives and if it has been successfully 'promoted'. He

maintains, however, that the ECU is a mediocre currency as it stands, less desirable than the Mark or even than certain others of its own component currencies, and the kind of monetary organization needed to make it a commercial success is not in existence. The author expands and develops his proposal for an extra-national composite currency unit which will have invariable purchasing power, a property that no other currency in history, not excluding gold, has ever had.

534 Monetary implication of the 1992 process.
Edited by Heidemarie Sherman.   London: Pinter, 1990. 256p.
The main question addressed by this volume is whether the close economic inter-relationships which already exist and are about to be intensified by the end of 1992 necessitate monetary union or not, and if so, how might union be achieved. The case-studies presented here bring hard facts to this emotive and controversial topic.

535 European monetary union.
Edited by M. T. Sumner, G. Zis.   London: Macmillan, 1982. 266p.
This book provides good background reading for those interested in European monetary integration. It covers a wide range of issues up to 1981.

536 On the meaning and future of the European Monetary System.
Tom de Vries.   Princeton, New Jersey: Princeton University Press, 1980. 60p.
A succinct appraisal by a central banker who served as director of the EC Commission and on the executive board of the International Monetary Fund (IMF), of the background and prospects for EMS at the beginning of the 1980s.

537 The Ecu and you.
London: Stoy Hayward, 1991. 4p.
The European Currency Unit is known as the ECU, and the fact that a medieval French coin was called the *écu* made the 3-letter abbreviation from the English language acceptable to the French. Only 4 pages, but the best and most accurate description there is of the ECU.

538 The Ecu report.
Michael Emerson, Christopher Huhne.   London: Pan Books in association with Sidgwick & Jackson, for the Commission of the European Communities, 1991. 224p.
This authoritative and highly readable book studies the benefits and costs of a single currency and looks into Europe's financial future. There is a foreword by Jacques Delors.

539 The European Monetary System.
Journal of Common Market Studies, vol. 27, no. 3 (March 1989). 157p.
A special issue marking ten years of the European Monetary System (EMS). Essays include discussion of the future of the EMS, models and strategies of economic integration, and the place of the EMS in the world order.

540 **European monetary union: a business perspective.**
London: Confederation of British Industry, 1989. 22p. (Report by the
CBI European Monetary Union Working Group).

The booklet explains the Confederation of British Industry's (CBI) policy stance on
matters relating to the European Exchange Rate Mechanism (ERM), European
Monetary Union (EMU) and the European Currency Unit (ECU).

541 **Everything you always wanted to know about monetary union but were
afraid to ask.**
Paris: Association for the Monetary Union of Europe, 1991. 24p.

This is a short, extremely clear and succinct guide to some of the issues raised by
European Monetary Union (EMU). The Association for the Monetary Union of
Europe (AMUE) was formed in 1987 as a focal point for businesses wishing to
contribute to the achievement and success of monetary union in Europe. Members
share the common vision of a Europe in which free passage of goods and services is
unfettered by the inconvenience, uncertainty and cost of multi-currency transactions.

542 **Paving the way: next steps for monetary cooperation in Europe and the
world.**
London: Federal Trust for Education and Research, 1987. 25p.

Report of a Federal Trust Study Group chaired by David Howell. It discusses closer
monetary integration in the EC and its interface with the evolving world monetary
situation.

Report on the activities of the Monetary Committee.
See item no. 580.

Budgets and taxation

543 **VAT in the European Community.**
A. Buckett. London: Butterworth, 1990. 176p.

A useful short survey of value-added tax in member states of the EC.

544 **Company tax harmonisation in the European Community.**
John Chown. London: Institute of Directors, 1989. 27p.

A short but readable pamphlet dealing with the complex problem of tax harmonization
in the EC.

545 **Corporate tax harmonisation and economic efficiency.**
Michael Devereux, Mark Pearson. London: Institute for Fiscal
Studies, 1989. 100p. (Report no. 35).

This report discusses the economic cost of differences in corporate taxes in the light of
harmonization proposals from the European Commission. The advent of the Single

European Market will remove barriers to business within the European Community, yet differences in corporate tax rates applied by the twelve member states will still exist. These differences mean that economic distortions will remain in Europe even after 1992. For example, firms may produce in the lowest-taxed country, rather than the lowest-cost country. Two pieces of evidence are presented on the scale of the problem: effective tax rates and incentives faced by companies investing in Europe are calculated; a survey of British companies describing the effect of tax on their international operations and their attitudes to harmonization is reported. Various options for reforms to the current situation are examined, with the objective of improving economic efficiency within Europe without prejudicing national political sovereignty.

546 British taxation and the Common Market.
Edited by Douglas Dosser. London: Charles Knight, 1973. 180p.
Here are seven essays dealing with the subject of fiscal harmonization. Harmonization has a three-fold purpose: to help free competition, to help economic union, and to provide revenue for the Community budget. The conclusion seems to be that harmonizing VAT is simple compared with all other types of taxation.

547 Taxes in the EEC and Britain. The problems of harmonization.
Douglas Dosser, S. S. Han. London: Chatham House and PEP, 1968. 46p.
By means of some carefully constructed tables the authors have shown much comparative material on taxation. They pinpoint some of the difficulties of harmonization and make a few suggestions on how the long-term objectives might be achieved.

548 Beyond 1992: a European tax system.
Edited by Malcolm Gammie, Bill Robinson. London: Institute of Fiscal Studies, 1989. 108p. bibliog. (Commentary no. 13).
This study is divided into chapters dealing with the Commission's view on a European tax system, the UK official response, an academic perspective, and the standpoint of the tax practitioner. It has a useful list of the draft directives of the Commission.

549 Towards 1992: harmonisation of indirect taxes.
F. Knox. London: Trade and Tariffs Research, 1990. 89p.
Describes the various types of taxes and why indirect taxes are of relevance to international trade. It sets out the General Agreement on Tariffs and Trade (GATT) and EC principles and gives details of cases concerning indirect taxes in the European Court of Justice. It pinpoints indirect taxes in the 1992 programme.

550 Guide to the 1989 general budget of the Commission of the European Communities and other Community institutions.
Edited by Michael O'Hagan. Aldershot, England: Dartmouth Publishing, 1989. 210p.
This guide gives full details of the budget for the European Commission and its associated institutions. It concentrates on the external spend – that is the money required for procurement of goods and services or for grants, loans and subsidies to

outside bodies – and it identifies and analyses all budget lines which are considered to represent opportunities for a wide variety of companies and organizations. The guide will be of value to those involved in supplying capital equipment and consumable goods, as well as to consultancies, construction companies, universities and training establishments, social and community workers, and research and development organizations.

551 **Fiscal harmonization in the European Community: national politics and international co-operation.**
Donald J. Puchala. London: Pinter, 1984. 158p.
Puchala tries to discover why policy-making in the European Community is such a lengthy process, using the introduction of value-added tax as an example. Members agree a general overall strategy but when this policy is taken back to the individual countries a long period of negotiation appears necessary to reach an area of compromise and consensus.

552 **Financing the European Community.**
Michael Shackleton. London: Pinter, 1990. 112p. (A Chatham House Paper).
Examines the implementation of the Delors agreement and subsequent decisions altering the institutional arrangements for implementing the EC budget. The paper also assesses the implications for the future financing of the EC.

553 **The European Community's priorities in tax policy.**
Stephen Smith. London: Institute of Fiscal Studies, 1990. 24p.
(Working Paper, no. 90/2).
This paper considers the rôle of the European Community in tax policy, and sets out some economic criteria for the division of responsibility for taxation between member states and the Community. The recent emphasis of EC policy on substantial harmonization of indirect taxes, including close approximation of VAT and duty rates, may have given undue weight to the remaining distortions in this area. The most important priorities for Community tax policy are, increasingly, the taxation of companies and individual investment, where major potential still exists for tax-induced distortion of industrial competitiveness and location decisions.

554 **Budgetary policies: the finances of the European Community.**
Helen Wallace. London: Allen & Unwin, for the University Association of Contemporary European Studies, 1980. 120p.
The author's aim was 'to clarify the discussion of budgetary policies with the EC and to relate them to broader analytical approaches'. Despite being short, the book achieves its objective of explaining why budgetary policy remains so rudimentary – it is because of the political controversies it generates over contributions, control and allocation. This is, however, a highly condensed book.

Inventory of taxes.
See item no. 591.

European
Communities
Publications

General

555 **The documentation of the European Communities: a guide.**
Ian Thomson.   London: Mansell, 1989. 382p.

This is *not* a European Community publication, but it is the clue to all the massive EC
output of documentation which reaches close on 3,000 individual copies a year. It is a
triumph of editing because, although the range of publications is so vast, Thomson
manages to describe even the most dismal pamphlet in such a way that it shows how
that publication relates to other aspects of EC activities. Because of the vast output of
the EC printing machines it was decided that for this bibliography only major
publications should be listed. *The documentation of the European Communities*,
therefore, becomes a useful companion. All reference books become out-of-date fairly
quickly, but Thomson also publishes *European Access* (q.v.) and this is also essential
for those engaged in research using EC documentation.

556 **Agreements and other bilateral commitments linking the Communities
with non-member countries.**
Luxembourg: Office for the Official Publications of the European
Communities (OOPEC), 1981– . twice a year.

This directory of international legal commitments linking the European Communities
to third countries or groups of third countries has two purposes: to provide a complete
list of Community agreements in force, and to give exact references to these
agreements so that the texts of documents can easily be found.

557 **The agricultural situation in the Community.**
Luxembourg: OOPEC, 1975– . annual.

Each volume has a detailed contents section but no index. The detailed contents for the statistical section is at the beginning of that section, in the middle of the volume. The report is published at the beginning of each calendar year and is often available a little before the parallel *General report* (q.v.).

558 **Bulletin of the European Communities.**
Luxembourg: OOPEC. monthly.

A monthly bulletin which reports on the activities of the Commission and the other Community institutions. It is edited by the Secretariat-General of the Commission and published in all official Community languages. The *Bulletin* is issued as a means of informing the public of EC developments in a comprehensive but concise form. Although compiled by the Commission it does outline explicitly the activities of the other EC institutions month by month. There is a supplement in a separate series published at irregular intervals. Each *Supplement* covers a single topic. The aim of the series would seem to be to give greater publicity to a Commission initiative, programme, report or proposal than would be the case if it were only summarized in the *Bulletin*.

559 **Comparative tables of the social security schemes in the member states of the European Communities.**
Luxembourg: OOPEC, 1961– . every two years, last edition 1990.

The volume contains information on financing, health care, sickness – cash benefits, maternity, invalidity, old age, survivors, employment injuries and occupational diseases, family benefits, and unemployment.

560 **Compendium of Community monetary texts.**
Luxembourg: OOPEC, 1981– . irregular.

This publication gathers together all the legal texts that are of most relevance to the work of the Monetary Committee. These are listed under the following headings: extracts from the Treaty founding the European Economic Community (including the Single European Act, 1986); coordination of economic policies; economic and monetary union; European Monetary System (EMS); capital movements; ECU and agricultural unit of account; committees (including the decision setting up and rules of procedure of the Economic Policy Committee).

561 **Compendium of Community provisions on social security.**
Luxembourg: OOPEC, 1981– . irregular, last edition 1986.

The *Compendium* brings together the official texts, with commentary, relating to social security for migrant workers. It contains the details of the basic EEC Regulations 1408/71 and 574/72 and subsequent amendments, the judgments of the Court of Justice and the decisions and recommendations of the Administrative Commission with regard to social security for migrant workers.

562   **Competition law in the EEC and in the ECSC.**
       Luxembourg: OOPEC, 1972– . irregular.
This book contains all the EC regulations in the area of competition in force at the time of compilation.

563   **Corps Diplomatique accrédité auprès des Communautés Européennes.**
       (Diplomatic Corps accredited to the European Communities.)
       Luxembourg: OOPEC, 1962– . twice a year.
The directory is arranged alphabetically by country. Under each country the address of the embassy is given, along with the names, rank and addresses of the key staff, and the date of their accreditation. There is a list of accredited countries in order of formal diplomatic precedence and a list of national days for the accredited countries. It is available only in French.

564   **The Courier.**
       Brussels: Commission of the European Communities, 1970– .
       bi-monthly.
Aimed at the non-specialist reader, the features and articles represent one of the most accessible introductions to European Community–Third World relations. In addition to general news and statements each issue covers a particular topic in some detail.

565   **Directory of higher education institutions.**
       Luxembourg: OOPEC, 1984. 200p.
The aim of the directory is to encourage contacts between academic institutions of higher education in the member states. In essence it is a directory of addresses of higher education institutions. For each member state the following information is given: organization of higher education, list of individual institutions with their contact address and the main academic subjects covered, other useful addresses, bibliography.

566   **ERASMUS Newsletter.**
       Luxembourg: OOPEC, 1982– . twice a year.
The function of *ERASMUS Newsletter* is to report on the developments in the European Community Action Scheme for the Mobility of University Students (ERASMUS). This involves news articles, case-studies of existing programmes, reports and announcements of conferences, and practical advice on the setting up and sustaining of contacts amongst academic institutions in the member states.

567   **Euro-info.**
       Luxembourg: OOPEC, 1985– . irregular.
This title is issued by the Task Force on Small and Medium-Sized Enterprises which aims to keep small businesses and the craft trade informed of EC developments of interest to them.

568   **Europa Transport: Observation of the transport markets: annual report.**
       Luxembourg: OOPEC, 1981– . annual.
This report is mainly a statistical publication, broken down between the different forms of transport.

569 **The European Community international organizations and multilateral agreements.**
Luxembourg: OOPEC, 1977. 180p.

The European Community, being a unique organization in international law, has had to develop its relations with other international bodies very carefully and in a piecemeal fashion. This title outlines the history of that development and lists in a systematic way the agreements between the EC and other international organizations.

570 **European Economy.**
Luxembourg: OOPEC, 1978– . irregular.

European Economy is the key journal for disseminating to the general public information regarding the economic policy of the EC and the member states.

571 **European University News.**
Luxembourg: OOPEC, 1965– . bi-monthly.

Each issue usually contains the following features: news of European studies – new courses and activities of associations of EC studies, for example, results of research projects; reports of conferences and seminars; calendar of future conferences, courses, seminars, etc.; brief review of new publications.

572 **The general report on the activities of the European Communities.**
Luxembourg: OOPEC, 1968– . annual.

The *General report* is broken down into chapters and sections. The broad headings are as follows: Review of the Community for the previous twelve months; Community institutions and financing; Financing Community activities; External relations; and Community law.

573 **Green Europe: Newsletter of the Common Agricultural Policy.**
Luxembourg: OOPEC, 1963– . irregular.

Each issue is devoted to a single topic relating to the Common Agricultural Policy. Titles include: *Milk: problem child of European agriculture*; *EEC food imports: the New Zealand file*; *Wine in the eighties*; *Aspects of the Common Agricultural Policy of concern to consumers*; *Community food aid*; *Food surpluses: disposal for welfare purposes*; and *Competition policy in agriculture*.

574 **Information on agriculture.**
Luxembourg: OOPEC, 1976– . irregular.

This was a series of studies on a wide range of topics undertaken by outside organizations and researchers on behalf of the Commission. Titles include: *Factors influencing ownership, tenancy, mobility and use of farmland in the United Kingdom*; *Potato products: production and markets in the EC*; *Cold storage warehousing in the EC – an inter-country comparison*; and *Energy consumption per tonne of competing agricultural products available in the EC*.

575 **Official Journal of the European Communities.**
Luxembourg: OOPEC, 1951– . daily.

The *Official Journal* is the authoritative source for all EC legislation. It also gives information on many of the activities of the EC institutions including various stages in the legislative and judicial processes. Finally, it gives details of calls to tender for public supply and public works contracts. It is published in all the official Community languages and is made up of distinct parts issued separately: Legislation; Information and notices; Supplement; Debates of the European Parliament; and Index. It comprises half of the total output from OOPEC. Taking all language versions together, the total print run is over 19,000,000 copies.

576 **Practical guide to the use of the European Communities' scheme of Generalized Tariff Preferences.**
Luxembourg: OOPEC, 1977– . annual (except 1985).

The Generalized System of Preferences (GSP) is an international scheme that allows developing countries to send products to the industrialized countries and not incur customs charges. The first Community GSP was introduced in 1971 and it has been maintained, with revisions, ever since.

577 **Report on competition policy.**
Luxembourg: OOPEC, 1972– . annual.

A resolution from the European Parliament in 1971 asked the Commission to make a special report each year on the development of competition policy, which was considered an integral element in the means of achieving the aims of the treaties establishing the European Communities. The report is published in conjunction with the *General report* (q.v.). The layout of the *Report on competition policy* has remained fairly constant, and headings include: General competition policy; Competition policy towards enterprises; Competition policy and government assistance to enterprises; The development of concentration, competition and competitiveness; and Annexes. These last give the decisions and rulings made by the Commission and Court of Justice during the year. Bibliographical references are given for certain categories. A list of studies commissioned from outside research institutes published during the year is also given.

578 **Report on social developments.**
Luxembourg: OOPEC, 1958– . annual.

From 1958 until 1978 the title was *Report on the development of the social situation in the European Community*. Like the *General report* (q.v.), this report is published annually as a result of a treaty obligation. The layout is as follows: Introduction; Social developments in the Community in the year under review; and a Statistical appendix with brief tables on Population, Education, Employment, Unemployment, Working conditions, Wages – labour costs, Standard of living, and Social protection.

579 **Report on the activities of the Economic Policy Committee.**
Luxembourg: OOPEC, 1986– . annual.

The report surveys the main activities of the Committee, lists its members, and gives the text of various statements, opinions and reports made during the year under review.

580 **Report on the activities of the Monetary Committee.**
Luxembourg: OOPEC, 1961– . annual.
Regular features that appear are a report on the general situation, a report on the activities of the Committee and the EC, and a list of members and their alternates of the Monetary Committee.

581 **Social Europe.**
Luxembourg: OOPEC, 1983– . bi-monthly.
The main EC source for background on the many facets of social and employment policy. Each issue gives quasi-official comment and overviews on current issues in the area, with up-dates on employment policy in each member state. A varying number of supplements each year give more detail and depth to the topics.

582 **University research on European integration.**
Luxembourg: OOPEC, 1980– . irregular.
This major bibliography is divided into two parts and gives lists of studies – arranged in alphabetical order of authors' names under the headings in the classification plan; a distinction is made between studies in progress, completed studies and published studies, and indexes – a directory of addresses, authors, research directors.

583 **Women of Europe.**
Luxembourg: OOPEC, 1978– . five times a year.
Each issue gives news and background on women's issues in a Community context, and Community issues from women's perspectives. A small number of supplements each year take topics for more detailed treatment. *Women in Europe* is a newsletter from the Commission's London Office with a similar, but less detailed treatment. In addition, there is a supplement to *Women of Europe* and about 30 titles have been published. These include *Community law and women* (1985); *European women in paid employment: their perception of discrimination at work* (1985); *Elections to the European Parliament: women and voting* (1985); *Community law and women* (1987); and *Men and women of Europe in 1987* (1987).

Euratom

584 **Euratom Supply Agency: annual report.**
Luxembourg: OOPEC, 1958– . annual.
The Euratom Supply Agency was established by the Treaty of Rome 1957, which set up the European Atomic Energy Community (Euratom). The Euratom Supply Agency is a part of the Commission. Its function is to ensure the supply of ores, source materials and special fissile materials to all users of such materials. A brief report on the activities of the Euratom Supply Agency on a year-by-year basis can be found in the 'Energy' section of the *General report on the activities of the European Communities* (q.v.). The following features have been standard since 1984: main activities of the supply agency; the development of nuclear energy in the Community;

supply of nuclear material and enrichment services in the EC; supply of other fuel cycle services; international agreements between Euratom and supplier states; administrative report.

Eurostat

585 ACP – basic statistics.
Luxembourg: OOPEC, 1981– . annual.

This paperback, issued by Eurostat (Statistical Office of the European Communities), provides basic information on the African, Pacific and Caribbean (ACP) countries: it includes essential data in the form of a selection of the most important statistics of the countries which have signed the Lomé III Convention with the Community. The Mediterranean countries which have association agreements with the Community are also included. The information covers the following fields: population, national accounts, industrial, mining and agricultural production, external trade, prices, finance, external aid, and standard of living. The publication is divided into four sections: the ACP in the world; the main economic and social indicators for each ACP state; the activities of the European Development Fund (EDF) and the European Investment Bank (EIB) under Lomé III; and the Mediterranean countries.

586 Basic statistics of the Community.
Luxembourg: OOPEC, 1960– . annual.

This is the most useful of the publications of the Statistical Office of the European Community (Eurostat) for the general reader. It is a paperback, pocket-sized, intended for the non-specialist, and includes statistics for Canada, Japan, USA, USSR and several non-EC European countries. Statistics cover the following fields: national accounts, regional accounts, finance, balance of payments, prices, population, education and training, employment, social protection, energy, iron and steel, agriculture, forestry and fisheries (production, consumption, balances, structure, prices and economic accounts), foreign trade, services, and transport.

587 Energy in Europe.
Luxembourg: OOPEC, 1968– . three times a year.

Energy in Europe aims to help the interested layman and specialist keep abreast of EC activities and policies in the area of energy policy and to show the short-, medium- and long-term energy outlook of the Community. The first part of the journal is devoted to articles usually summarizing major Commission studies. In the latter part there are short items relating to recent Community activities in the energy field.

588 European Regional Development Fund: annual report.
Luxembourg: OOPEC, 1975– . annual.

Standard features of each report include co-ordination of regional policies, European Regional Development Fund operations for the year, specific Community regional development measures, the European Regional Development Fund from 1975 to date, statistical data, and a bibliography.

589 **Eurostat Review.**
Luxembourg: OOPEC, 1987– . annual.
EC statistics are given to show trends over a ten-year period.

590 **Financial report of the European Coal and Steel Community.**
Luxembourg: OOPEC, 1956– . annual.
The *Financial report* records the borrowing and lending of the Commission in the area covered by the ECSC Treaty.

591 **Inventory of taxes.**
Luxembourg: OOPEC, 1970– . irregular.
This inventory of taxes levied by the state and local authorities in the member states is a major reference source of factual information. It does not attempt to draw comparisons or analyse the various tax systems.

592 **Investment in the Community coalmining and iron and steel industries.**
Luxembourg: OOPEC, 1956– . annual.
This report is prepared on the basis of a regular survey of investment in the EC coal and steel industries. The survey collects information on actual and forecast capital expenditure and on the production potential of coal and steel enterprises. There are detailed sections on the coalmining industry, coking plants, iron-ore mines, and the iron and steel industry.

593 **State of the environment.**
Luxembourg: OOPEC, 1977– . irregular.
The aim of these reports is to explain some of the activities undertaken by the EC with regard to the environment. They have chapters on urban and industrial activities and on agriculture, forestry and fishing; they give details of the state of the environment in the air, on land, in inland waters and the sea. There are also articles on wildlife and analyses of the economic implications of environmental policy.

Council of Ministers

594 **Review of the work of the Council of Ministers.**
Luxembourg: OOPEC, 1962– . annual.
Chapter headings in the review include: freedom of movement and common rules, economic and social policy, external relations and relations with the associated states, agriculture, fisheries, and administrative matters. It is possible to find out the number of days spent on Council meetings and meetings of preparatory bodies, the number of instances when the Council was involved in cases brought before the Court of Justice, and the number of questions received by the Council from the European Parliament.

European Parliament

595 **European Parliament bibliography 1970–1978.**
Luxembourg: OOPEC, 1979.

This is an index of non-EC sources of information about the European Parliament, although some EC publications are listed. The material is indexed under such headings as procedures and rules, sessions and activities, and direct elections. Annual supplements are published.

596 **Official handbook of the European Parliament.**
Luxembourg: European Parliament, 1980– . irregular.

This handbook contains biographies of the Members (MEPs), committee and group membership, and a directory of personnel in the secretariat of the European Parliament.

597 **Rules of procedure.**
Luxembourg: European Parliament, 1981– . irregular.

This booklet gives the rules of procedure adopted by the European Parliament in 1981 and subsequently. It includes changes brought about by the Single European Act.

Economic and Social Committee

598 **Annual report of the Economic and Social Committee.**
Luxembourg: OOPEC, 1973– . annual.

The function of the Economic and Social Committee (usually abbreviated to ECOSOC) is to advise the Commission and Council of the views of the interest groups involved on Community proposals and matters of its own concern. Its annual report contains information on the rôle and influence of ECOSOC, press relations and outside reactions, participation in meetings outside the Committee, personnel changes, internal affairs of the General Secretariat, a list of opinions, studies and information reports issued, and a list of opinions drawn up by ECOSOC on its own initiative since 1973. There is no index.

Court of Justice

599 **Synopsis of the work of the Court of Justice of the European
Communities.**
Luxembourg: OOPEC, 1980– . annual.
The Court is the legal guardian of the Treaties and has had, and will have in the future,
considerable importance in the development of the Community. The synopsis gives a
detailed breakdown of the case law of the Court during the year; this includes both a
description of the major cases and also a statistical section, a description of the work of
the departments of the Court of Justice (Registry, Library, Research and Documentation Division, Translation Directorate, Interpretation Division), a list of the judges of
the Court, information and documentation on the Court of Justice and its work, a list
of journals published in EC countries which cover Community case law, a list of Press
and Information Offices of the European Communities, organization of public sittings
of the Court, a summary of types of procedure, and notes for the guidance of counsel
at oral hearings.

Court of Auditors

600 **Court of Auditors of the European Communities.**
Luxembourg: OOPEC, 1988– . irregular.
The Court of Auditors was established by the Treaty of Brussels in 1975 and became
operative in 1977. Its work is to audit the accounts of the Community institutions. This
is a short pamphlet giving details of the powers, work, principal reports, structure and
responsibilities of the members of the Court of Auditors.

Consultative Committee of the European Coal and Steel Community (ECSC)

601 **Handbook of the Consultative Committee of the ECSC.**
Luxembourg: OOPEC. irregular.
This handbook contains the following information: the text of the various treaties and
regulations that relate to the Consultative Committee, the composition and
organization of the Consultative Committee since its formation, the current
organization and composition of the Consultative Committee, and an annexe
containing a list of the publications of the Consultative Committee.

European Bureau for Lesser Used Languages

602 **Contact Bulletin.**
Dublin: European Bureau for Lesser Used Languages, 1983– . ten
issues a year.

This journal reports on the activities of the Bureau, seminars and conferences, EC
activities in the area of minority languages and cultures, and other items of general
interest.

Vocational training

603 **Annual report of European Centre for the Development of Vocational
Training.**
Berlin: European Centre for the Development of Vocational Training,
1976– . annual.

The report gives details of the publications programme for the year, visitors to the
Centre, the study visit programme and other continuing activities; a description of the
activities undertaken during the year in question in the Centre's current main areas of
interest, the Centre's relations with EC institutions and other organizations; manpower
and financial resources; list of meetings held; membership of the Management Board
and the Centre's personnel; list of publications issued during the year, including
language and number of copies printed. The Centre also publishes *Vocational Training*
three times a year.

European Community Action Programme

604 **Programme News.**
Brussels: European Community Action, 1984– . irregular.

There have been two Action Programmes which aim to help with the transition of
young people from education to adult and working life, as well as a number of working
documents. In the first there were twenty-eight projects and in the second thirty.
Programme News promotes the activities of the Action Programme and announces
details of publications.

European Foundation for the Improvement of Living and Working Conditions

605 **Annual report of the European Foundation for the Improvement of Living and Working Conditions.**
Luxembourg: OOPEC, for the Foundation, 1976– . annual.
The Foundation became an autonomous Community organization in 1975 and its annual report contains a description of the work programme for the year; a breakdown of the programme into topics and a description of work undertaken; evaluation activities; publications of the European Foundation; meetings organized by the European Foundation; the budget; and a directory of members of the Administrative Board, the Committee of Experts, Foundation staff and of research bodies and experts involved in implementing the work programme for the year.

European Investment Bank

606 **Annual report of the European Investment Bank.**
Luxembourg: EIB, 1958– . annual.
The European Investment Bank (EIB) was established under the Treaty of Rome and its annual report contains the following regular features: names and national position of the Board of Governors, the Audit Committee, Board of Directors, the Management Committee and the organizational structure of the Bank; financing provided in the year under review; operations within the Community; operations outside the Community; resources; results for the year; administration, financial statements; historical pattern of financing.

European University Institute

607 **Academic Year.**
Florence: EUI. annual.
This is the annual prospectus of the European University Institute (EUI) in Florence and contains details of the administrative organization of the EUI, academic organization, admission procedures, work methods and organization of studies, degrees offered, Jean Monnet Fellowships, services for research students (visiting professors, library, computing facilities, study travel, linguistic assistance, publications, vocational guidance, etc.), practical information, and a list of national grant-award bodies – each language version of the prospectus has an additional section on grants relevant to native speakers of that language.

608   **Report of activities of the EUI.**
Luxembourg: OOPEC, 1976– . annual.

The annual report of the European University Institute gives details of officers and full-time staff of the Institute, research and teaching activities (including running projects, future research, activities during the year in question and the work of the Jean Monnet Fellows), the Jean Monnet Fellows, activities of the Institute's authorities, and other activities of the Institute.

Youth Forum of the European Communities

609   **Youth Opinion.**
Brussels: Youth Forum, 1982– . quarterly.

The aim of the Youth Forum is to increase the activities and the actions which will ensure the greater involvement of youth in the future development of the European Communities; to increase their rôle in the development of mutual understanding and safeguarding the equal rights of all citizens in the European Communities; to increase democracy and real participation at all levels of the European Communities. *Youth Opinion* is the journal of the Forum.

Periodicals

610 **Business Europe.**
Maldon, England: Bower House, 1990– . 10 times a year.
A very practical journal dealing in facts rather than theories.

611 **Economic policy – a European forum.**
Edited by Georges de Ménil, Richard Portes. Cambridge, England:
Cambridge University Press, 1985– . bi-annually.
A good source of analysis of economic affairs. Its coverage is wider than just EC
activities.

612 **Energy in Europe.**
Luxembourg: Office for Official Publications of the EC. 1985– . three
times a year.
A valuable EC-produced journal for any specialist in this field. It reviews market
developments, policy trends, EC initiatives, and research and development programmes in energy.

613 **Euroednews.**
London: UK Centre for European Education, 1980– . bi-annually.
This is the organ of the UK Centre for European Education, one of fifteen national
centres in Western European countries (twelve from the Community plus Austria,
Sweden and Switzerland). All are linked together through an International Centre for
European Education. The UK centre was established by the Department of Education
and Science in 1978, primarily to introduce and develop the teaching of European
awareness in British schools.

Periodicals

614 European Affairs.
Amsterdam: Elsevier, 1987– . quarterly.

European Affairs is a magazine in which prominent Europeans and non-Europeans voice their opinions regarding Europe and its impact on political and business relations. It also publishes unique statistical and economic indicators concerning gross national product, balance of payments, consumer purchasing power and economic forecasts.

615 European Business Journal.
London: Whurr, 1989– . quarterly.

The *European Business Journal* provides an independent forum for the presentation and discussion of the major issues affecting business in the European Community.

616 European Business Review.
Bradford, England: MCB University Press, 1989– . quarterly.

Each issue contains an in-depth examination of the business structure and opportunities of EC countries, a comparative analysis of management know-how in action across Europe, focusing on acquisitions and mergers, manufacturing, quality assurance and management development.

617 European Environment.
Shipley, England: European Research Press, 1991– . six times a year.

Throughout Europe environmental concerns have come to the forefront of public and political debate in recent years. *European Environment* examines in depth issues of environmental importance in a European context, presenting the latest information and research from around Europe in a concise and accessible way. With regular country, market and issue profiles, this journal can also offer a detailed, factual and objective analysis of issues of widespread interest and implication, with an emphasis on useful practical information.

618 European Research.
Edited by Jonathan Wilson. Shipley, England: European Research Press, 1990– . six times a year.

Contains well-written reports on current research into European affairs.

619 Facts on File.
New York; Oxford: Facts on File, 1941– . weekly.

This world news digest gives good coverage of EC affairs. There is a cumulative index and maps.

620 Journal of Common Market Studies.
Edited by Peter Robson. Oxford: Blackwell, 1962– . quarterly.

This journal is amongst the foremost vehicles for the transmission of academic ideas and research on the processes, institutions, and practicalities of European integration. As a consequence, it offers a very wide range of topics, often giving very considerable detail in certain areas. The articles, almost always authoritative, must be carefully read, for they do not offer quick answers. Each issue also contains serious scholarly reviews of recent publications.

621 **Journal of World Trade.**
Edited by Jacques Werner. Geneva, Switzerland: Werner, 1988– . bi-monthly.

The *Journal of World Trade* (published as *Journal of World Trade Law*, 1967–88) reaches beyond the EC in its coverage. However, given the nature of the EC as a major trading bloc, this is a good source of serious academic comment and modelling on the international economics of the Community. Under its former title more emphasis was given to legal aspects and trade law.

622 **Keesing's Record of World Events.**
Harlow, England: Longman, 1987– . monthly.

Keesing's has covered EC affairs thoroughly since the signing of the Treaty of Rome. It is based on constant monitoring of the world's press and information sources and there is linkage to other news items. Earlier events are clearly signposted and there is a cumulative index. It was published as *Keesing's Contemporary Archives* from 1931 to 1986.

623 **Lawyers in Europe.**
Edited by Joanna Hicks. London: Professional & Business Information, 1990– . six times a year.

This review is produced in response to an increasing demand for information on the changing shape of the legal professions and legal practice in Europe, and provides regular information, commentary and advice.

624 **Marketing in Europe.**
London: Economist Intelligence Unit, 1970– . monthly.

An information and research bulletin dealing with consumer goods markets, marketing and distribution in continental Europe. It concentrates on France, Italy, West Germany, Belgium–Luxembourg and the Netherlands, but contains occasional studies on other countries.

625 **New European.**
Edited by John Coleman. London: New European Publications, in association with the Centre for European Studies, 1987– . quarterly.

New European is distinctive in that it considers all of Europe, not just the Community and its institutions but also the Council of Europe, the European Free Trade Association (EFTA) and the Nordic Council, as well as, of course, Eastern Europe. It is a platform for European leaders to put forward their views about the future of Europe in the fields of culture, environment, politics, business and finance.

Periodicals

626 **Public Policy and Administration.**

Edited by Barry J. O'Toole. London: Joint University Council, RIPA, Regent's College, 1986– . 3 editions a year.

Publishes articles on EC affairs from time to time but the Spring 1991 edition was a special issue called 'Britain and the evolving European Community'. It contains contributions by Howard Elcock, Ken Harrop, Brian Bender, Juliet Lodge and Frank Gregory. The journal was first published as *PAC Bulletin* in 1964, subsequently became *Public Administration Bulletin*, and changed to the current title in 1986.

627 **Trade Union Information Bulletin.**

Edited by Alan Burnett. Brussels: Commission of the European Communities, 1985– . bi-monthly.

Independently edited, although officially produced, this newsletter is a valuable source of accessible short articles on topics in social and employment policy at an EC level.

628 **World Today.**

Edited by Christopher Cviic. London: Royal Institute for International Affairs, 1945– . monthly.

Although concerned with wider world affairs, this publication can offer a useful range of EC-related articles. Articles are shorter than usual for the academic press, and the journal's reaction time to world events is often commendably quick. Authors include not only academics but political figures and specialists from many viewpoints, offering a valuable spread of insight and ideas suitable for any serious interest.

Directories

Atlases

629 **Atlas of Europe: a profile of Western Europe.**
Robert M. Croucher, John C. Bartholomew, John McLachan, Malcolm
C. Macdonald. Edinburgh: John Bartholomew; London: Frederick
Warne, 1974. 128p.

Although this atlas is old it is worth studying, and much of the information is valid in
the 1990s. Its aims are to set out a series of clear, definite statements about Western
Europe and the quality of life that its people enjoy. The atlas breaks new ground in the
way that geographical data are presented.

630 **An atlas of EEC affairs.**
Ray Hudson, David Rhind, Helen Mounsey. London: Methuen,
1984. 158p.

An account of regional economic, social and demographic developments. 'Atlas' is a
bit of a misnomer but it does contain maps and tables and is very clearly produced.

Dictionaries

631 **A dictionary of the European Communities.**
John Paxton. London: Macmillan, 1982. 2nd ed. 282p.

The second edition of this encyclopaedic dictionary has over 900 entries ranging from
AASM to Zollverein, with coverage of such varied topics as historical attempts at
European unification, economic profiles of different countries, abbreviations and
acronyms, a précis of the major treaties (Rome, Paris, Accessions and Euratom), and

even wine consumption within the Community. A dictionary, who's who and gazetteer, all in one. No longer up to date, but it contains much information not easily found elsewhere. The first edition (*A Dictionary of the European Economic Community*, 1977) was commended by the Library Association's Committee for the McColvin Medal as an outstanding reference book.

632 **Eurojargon: a dictionary of EC acronyms, abbreviations and sobriquets.**
Anne Ramsay. Stamford, England: Capital Planning Information, 1991. 3rd ed. 85p.

The dictionary is designed to clarify and explain the many acronyms, abbreviations and sobriquets which abound in the European Communities. It contains 1400 entries. It uses English translations throughout, except where the foreign abbreviation is in common use in the UK.

633 **Guide to EC acronyms and abbreviations.**
Brussels: Price Waterhouse, 1990. 32p.

In the preface, the director of EC services at Price Waterhouse says '. . . documents emanating from the European Commission can severely test the limits of comprehension'. They do indeed, and this pamphlet goes some way towards clarification.

Directories

634 **Grants from Europe: how to get money and influence policy.**
Ann Davison, Bill Seary. London: Bedford Square Press, 1990. 6th ed. 132p.

The sixth edition of this book has been completely revised and expanded to take account of the Single European Act, the free internal market of 1992 and People's Europe Initiatives. It is clearly arranged and gives up-to-date information on key contacts in Brussels and the UK, including addresses and telephone numbers, how to apply for grants and how to assess the chances of success, what problems to expect along the way, and key publications. There are chapters covering the following categories of funding: unemployment, women, ethnic minority groups, people with disabilities, the environment, the Third World, education and culture, and consumer interests. Although targeted at the voluntary sector, this highly practical work is of potential value to any group or company seeking EC funding.

635 **Doing business in the European Community.**
John Drew. London: Whurr, 1991. 3rd ed. 300p.

This book – written by the head of the UK offices of the Commission of the European Communities and visiting professor of European management at the Management School, Imperial College, London – provides a framework for managers involved in developing European strategies and is a practical guide and reference source on the European Community, and its institutions, policies and practices as they affect business. It also has sections on developing European strategies, exporting joint ventures, and other methods of collaboration within the European context. For ease and speed of use, there are over 100 short, boxed entries written by experts, commissioners, parliamentarians, and businessmen, which provide checklists of the main points relevant to each topic discussed.

636 **Western European economic organizations: a comprehensive guide.**
Robert Fraser.   Harlow, England: Longman, 1991. 400p.

Each organization with influence on economic policy-making is described and its impact on economic affairs assessed. These include central banks, government agencies, regulatory bodies, stock exchanges, and a wide range of political, industrial, labour, academic and campaigning organizations. A typical entry provides full contact details, principal officers, organizational structure, funding, aims and objectives, rôle in national and economic policy-making, history, affiliations, and publications. To help understand the political and economic context for each organization, information is given on each country, including its constitutional framework, the pattern of government since 1945, an outline of economic development since 1945, the structure of industrial organization, and an overview of government economic policy-making.

637 **The European buy-out directory.**
Josephine Grierson.   London: Pitman, 1990. 350p.

This directory offers a comprehensive listing of firms in the field of leveraged management buy-outs and buy-ins. It has been designed to provide all the contacts needed to assemble a financial and professional team.

638 **EEC contacts.**
Jim Hogan.   Newbury, England: Eurofi, 1987. 3rd ed. 200p.

A directory of contacts for the European Community and EEC-related questions is a compendium of information sources within UK government departments, EEC institutions in Brussels and Luxembourg, and other trade-related contacts throughout the Community. It is primarily intended for the business community and is arranged by subject, to direct the user quickly and easily to the primary sources of information.

639 **The European marketplace.**
James Hogan, foreword by Sir Leon Brittan.   London: Macmillan,
1990. 600p. bibliog.

The European marketplace simplifies the task for directors of companies of all sizes, marketing and sales executives, accountants, lawyers and business consultants when enquiring into new developments across every conceivable business activity, from setting up a business in other European countries to introducing new training for their managers and workforce at home. It guides the readers into the information system via key contacts. Listing the references and contacts in the context of the changes taking place, this book brings together experts in industry, commerce, government, the professions, and the European Community in a wide-ranging survey of issues affecting the way business is done in the new Europe.

640 **EC funding for academic research.**
Michael Hopkins. Loughborough, England: European Research
Centre, Loughborough University, 1990. 58p.

A brief guide providing practical assistance to academic and research staff who want
information on EC research funding and how to make application for it.

641 **The Europe 1992 directory: a research and information guide.**
Edited by Anthony Inglis, Catherine Hoskyns. London: Her
Majesty's Stationery Office, 1990. 147p.

An essential reference for anyone who needs to keep up to date on developments in
the 1992 programme and the response of organizations from a variety of sectors.
Information is included on organizations, where to go and whom to contact; research
and training programmes; planning for businesses; and databases – what's available,
quality, cost and accessibility.

642 **The European Community 1991: a practical guide for business, media
and government.**
Edited by Brian Morris, Klaus Boehm, Maurice Geller. London:
Macmillan, 1990. 384p.

The first edition of *The European Community* was devised as a biennial practical guide
for business and government and was published in 1981. Designed for easy reference
and fully cross-referenced, it is aimed at anyone who has links with the EC, through
trade, travel, transport, the environment, consumer protection, employment, education, social affairs, overseas aid, foreign affairs, law, justice, industry, energy,
agriculture, finance, investment and marketing. It is also useful for those intending to
establish a business, or claiming grants and loans from European institutions; and for
people who are concerned in any way with European economic and political trends and
prospects. It is divided into three main parts: the European Community framework,
with diagrams explaining the structures of agriculture, budgetary processes, consumer
protection, education policy, environment policy, European institutions, external trade
policy, finance policy, harmonization policy, industrial policy, legislative processes of
the EC, regional policy, research policy, social policy, transport policy, work and
employment, telecommunications, broadcasting and technology; an A–Z of European
Community issues such as coal and steel (ECSC) financial aid, duty-free allowances,
energy, environment, European Investment Bank, external trade, farm fund,
harmonization, regional fund, self-employed, social fund; and finally, a European
directory giving details of the Secretariat of the European Parliament, the Council of
Ministers Secretariat, the Commission of the European Communities, the Members of
the European Parliament, and the Directory of Representative Organizations.

643 **European Community directory and diary.**
Edited by James O'Donnell, Dermot Scott. Dublin: Institute of
Public Administration, 1975.

Contains details of the institutions of the European Community and their associated
bodies and groups, a desk diary and a digest of historical, statistical and geographical
data on the Community, a glossary of Community terminology, and a Brussels street
map. Another useful work is *Chapmans European Directory* edited by Peter Kaye,
with a foreword by Sir John Harvey-Jones (London: Chapmans Publishers, 1991.
352p.). It gives the history of the European Community and explains the workings of

each of its institutions, from the Council of Ministers and the Court of Auditors to the functions of the directorates-general. The formation of policy and the decision-making processes are particularly attended to, together with résumés of agricultural, industrial and social policies, the European Monetary System and the activities of the European Investment Bank. It also contains a Who's Who of all the European Community's major players, from the president of the European Community, through the 17 commissioners and the 518 members of the European Parliament to the scores of committees and lesser officials. It is completely cross-referenced, listing hundreds of names, addresses, telephone and fax numbers, political affiliations and job descriptions. There are also contributions by Jacques Delors, Enrique Baron Crespo, Sir Fred Catherwood and Ernst Günther Broder.

644 **Hollis Europe.**
   Edited by Rosemary Sarginson. Sunbury-on-Thames, England: Hollis Directories, 1991. 2nd ed. 736p.

This directory, produced in association with the International Committee of Public Relations Consultancies Associations, contains eight sections covering twenty-six European countries, enabling the reader to identify new contacts and trace the links between client companies and their public relations consultancies. The skills index and resource register, with sixty pages of charts, enables clients to identify the consultancy in the right region with the specialization required. A typical consultancy entry provides essential information: contact name for international business; telephone, telex and fax numbers; and details of number of employees, fee income, clients, and any international networks that have been established.

645 **PMS Parliamentary Companion.**
   Lionel Zetter. London: PMS Publications, 1989– . quarterly.

Although two-thirds of this publication deals with UK parliamentary affairs, the section covering the European Community is extremely useful and lists members of the European Commission with their responsibilities, directorates-general and directors-general. There is also an alphabetical list of British MEPs with addresses, UK European constituencies with their MEPs, and an alphabetical list of MEPs by country. Committees of the European Parliament are listed.

646 **Annual review of European Community affairs 1990.**
   Oxford: Brassey's, for the Centre for European Policy Studies, 1990. 400p.

This annual review deals with the year 1989. Much happened in that year, including the take-off of economic and monetary union. These events are well recorded, as are progress on the internal market and external trade policy.

647 **Consumer Europe 1991.**
   London: Euromonitor, 1991. 350p.

This publication gives statistical data on over 250 consumer products across seventeen European markets. Data coverage runs from 1984 to 1989, with forecasts to 1994. It also has a special data section on Eastern Europe.

Directories.

648 **Directory of European Community trade and professional associations 1990.**
Brussels: Editions Delta, 1991. 4th ed. 464p.

The directory, an official publication of the European Communities, lists federations of associations of which the Commission of the European Communities has official cognizance. Listings are correlated within sectors of activity: industry, crafts, small and medium-sized enterprises, trade, transport, professions, other activities, trade unions, consumer and other organizations. A comprehensive reference work which includes some 500 trade and professional associations with a European or international membership, giving its name in each official language and the year of its inception. A total of 5,000 associations are included, showing chairman and general secretary, address, telephone and telex numbers, together with full details of national member organizations. It is trilingual in French, English and German.

649 **EEC brief.**
Lisburn, Northern Ireland: Locksley Press, 1991. 9th ed. 4 vols.

This is a practical, loose-leaf handbook for the business, professional and public sectors and covers institutions, contact points, free movement of goods, persons, services and capital, agriculture, fisheries, company law, competition law, transport, labour law, health and safety at work, environment, consumer protection, and all EC grants and loans.

650 **European business and industry 1990–91.**
Munich, Germany: Who's Who Edition, 1991. 2 vols.

In volume one of this directory there are more than 9,500 detailed biographies of Europe's leading executives; in volume two more than 1,400 full-length company profiles, with in-depth information on exports, imports, management and strategies. In a total of 2,900 pages it thus provides an overview of companies and managers, with some 4,000 quick-reference entries on corporate leaders in each sector and nation.

651 **The European Communities encyclopedia and directory 1992.**
London: Europa, 1991. 430p.

The European Communities encyclopedia and directory 1992 is both a survey and a directory, providing comprehensive details on the separate European Communities. The contents include an encyclopaedia of European organizations, acronyms and terms; member states of the Community; and politicians and others who have contributed to the development of the Communities and Community policy. Six essays analyse the political, economic, social and legal frameworks of the European Communities, 1992, and external affairs of the Communities. A statistical section, produced in collaboration with the Office for Official Publications of the European Communities, contains data covering all areas of the European Communities, including trade, employment and industrial production. The work concludes with an extensive directory containing up-to-date information on names and addresses, telephone, telex and fax numbers, and the principal officials of all the major Community organizations.

652 **European directory of business information libraries.**
London: Euromonitor, 1990. 208p.

A directory for business, financial and marketing researchers giving names of over 700 libraries, in seventeen European countries, with specialized business information and commercial reference services.

152

653   **European directory of marketing information sources.**

London: Euromonitor, 1991. 2nd ed. 400p.

A comprehensive guide to all major sources of marketing information in seventeen Western European countries. It includes government and official information sources, business and marketing journals, major business libraries and information databases, and features helpful business contacts such as chambers of commerce and commercial development agencies.

654   **European directory of trade and business organisations.**

London: Euromonitor, 1990. 293p.

In addition to the EC twelve, this directory covers Austria, Norway, Sweden and Switzerland, together with Pan-European organizations. Each entry gives full contact details for the organization, its aims, membership details, and its services and publications.

655   **European marketing data and statistics 1991.**

London: Euromonitor, 1991. 26th ed. 450p.

A report giving ten-year statistical data (1980–90) on economic, social and demographic subjects for all European countries both east and west.

656   **European municipal directory.**

Monmouth, Wales: European Directory, 1991. 1000p.

This directory lists all local authorities in twelve countries, giving name, postal address, telephone and fax numbers, political composition, population, names of the chief executive, the financial officer and the chairman or leader of the council. It also explains how local government works in the EC, and there are articles written by experts for each country, indicating the extent of local spending powers, ability to raise revenue, administrative responsibilities and electoral procedures.

657   **Guide to European business media.**

Wimbush, England: Grice Wheeler Business Communications, 1991.

three times a year.

This guide is a practical manual designed for use by those who need to disseminate news and information throughout Western Europe. It covers all member countries of the European Community, together with Austria, Norway, Sweden and Switzerland. Information is arranged by country. Within each country entry, listings are made of newspapers, magazines, news agencies, radio and television, in that order. Contact addresses for press cuttings agencies and embassies are also included. Addresses for the UK advertising agencies are listed at the back. The entries have been compiled from information provided by the organizations concerned and supplemented by the publishers' own research.

658   **Kompass.**

East Grinstead, England: Reed Information Services, 1962– .

Kompass directories are a valuable source of information on companies in EC member states. Each entry gives contact details, sales figures, number of employees, names of directors, and a description of the firm's products or services. The volumes which are available are: Belgium (29th ed., 24,000 companies); Denmark (31st., 16,300); France (58th, 96,000); Federal Republic of Germany (19th, 40,000); Ireland (5th, 10,000);

Directories

Italy (30th, 38,000); Luxembourg (12th, 1,700); Netherlands (27th, 24,000); Portugal (1st, 5,000); Spain (21st, 20,000); United Kingdom (3 vols, 42,000). Greece is not available. There is a database version which may be searched by specific company, sector, country and sales.

659 **1990 directory of EEC information sources.**

Genval, Belgium: Euroconfidentiel, 1990. 750p.

Who is responsible for aquaculture in the European Commission's DG XIV? What is the name and fax number of the secretary-general of the European Committee for Standardization? Which EEC database can provide figures on unemployment and foreign trade? Which law firm specializing in taxation can service its clients in Russian, Swedish, Greek or Japanese? These and many other questions are answered in this directory. It covers EC organizations, EC professional associations, law firms and consultants, press and news agencies and government bodies including diplomatic missions. The French-language edition is *Annuaire 90 des sources d'information communautaires.*

660 **Official European Communities information services in the United Kingdom and Republic of Ireland.**

Nottingham, England: European Information Association, 1991. 25p.

Lists, by county and town, all information services in the UK and Ireland which receive their information direct from the EC. The services included are: Commission and European Parliament offices, European Documentation Centres, EC Depository libraries, Euro Info Centres, European Reference Centres and EC Information Relays. Each type of service is defined, so that the user can determine what resources are available, and full contact details are provided for each information unit, together with information on the documentation held.

661 **Panorama of EC industry 1990.**

Luxembourg: Office of Official Publications of the EC, 1991. 1152p.

This annual publication gives an analysis of industry structure, prospects, trends in production, employment and trade for 168 sections of manufacturing and the service industries. It gives statistics from 1980 to 1988 or 1989, and forecasts up to 1991 for all major sections. In addition, there is a comparison of the EC figures with those of the US and Japan.

662 **Yearbook of the European Communities and of the other European organisations 1991.**

Brussels: Editions Delta, 1991. 11th ed. 480p.

A compendium of practical information, containing details about the institutions and bodies of the EC, including the European Parliament, Council and Commission, the Court of Justice and the Court of Auditors, the European Investment Bank and the Economic and Social Committee. Details are given of their structure, operation, activities and establishment plans. There are data on the diplomatic corps, official EC publications, European studies, and European movements and associations. It is trilingual in French, English and German.

Bibliographies and Databases

663 Euro High Tech: a survey of non-official statistical sources in the field of high technology products in the member states.
Margaret Brittin, David Mort.   Stamford, England: Capital Planning Information, 1987. 141p.

This publication represents the results of a study to produce an inventory and detailed subject and country indexes of publications in the high-technology field that are not available through official sources. It is in general confined to statistical data which appear on a reasonably regular basis, although some 'one-off' reports have been included where these are particularly important or current. It covers trade and professional associations, market research organizations, management consultants, research institutes, trade journals, specialist publishers and companies. Among the sectors covered by the survey are EDP (electronic data processing) equipment (e.g. micros, minis and mainframe), telecommunications, consumer electronics, and medical and analytical equipment.

664 A reader's guide to Britain and the European Community.
Carol Ann Cosgrove.   London: Chatham House and PEP, 1970. 106p.

A useful guide which brings together details of books, journals, articles, press releases and official reports. The aim is to help the British public to decide about the advantages and disadvantages of membership of the EEC.

665 A survey of European Communities databases.
Terry Hanson.   *ASLIB Proceedings*, vol. 42, no. 6 (June 1990), p. 171–88.

Written by an authority on online systems – the author is Databases Officer for the European Information Association – this lists and gives details of all EC-produced databases, or those with a significant EC content available in the UK.

666   **On line to Europe: a guide to EC databases.**
Elizabeth Hardt.   *Europe*, 270 (Oct. 1987), p. 21–7.
A brief but reliable introduction to EC databases.

667   **Policy formation in the European Communities: a bibliographical guide to Community documentation.**
Michael Hopkins.   London: Mansell, 1981. 339p.
The author, who has acted as a consultant to the Commission on information matters, reviews the making of policy in the major areas of activity, with detailed references and abstracts of major documents.

668   **Europe 1992: sources of information in the UK.**
Isabelle Igert.   London: Whurr, 1990. 100p.
This book aims to provide a guide to the various sources of information available in the UK. The twelve chapters of the book cover offices for the EC in the UK, the UK parliament, government departments, European documentation centres (EDCs), depository libraries, European reference centres, Euro Info centres (EICs), business innovation centres, chambers of commerce, associations, consultants, and the media. The book explains the rôle of each of the organizations included, as well as providing details of how each may be contacted and listing any publications produced. A concluding section gives basic documentation on EEC matters for those making contact with EC countries for the first time.

669   **The European Community: bibliographic excursions.**
Edited by Juliet Lodge.   London: Pinter, 1983. 259p.
A collection of well-written and accessible essays on the major areas of EC activity. The essays themselves, by academics and EC workers, serve as a context for extensive and well-researched bibliographies.

670   **European Communities information.**
Anne Ramsay.   Newcastle-under-Lyme, England: AAL Publishing, 1990. 30p.
Aimed primarily at information workers, this is nevertheless a clear and practical introduction to the information produced by the EC for any reader. It lists and describes key titles and bibliographical tools.

671   **Eurostat index.**
Anne Ramsay.   Stamford, England: Capital Planning Information, 1989. 4th ed. 304p.
The compiler has indexed over 150 titles in the Eurostat series of statistical tables produced by the Statistical Office of the European Community. It takes the form of an alphabetical keyword index to the contents of these tables, with hundreds of references and cross-references. Each Eurostat title is briefly described in the introduction to the index. It will not answer 'How many children are in the nursery schools in Italy?' or 'What percentage of houses in Crete have a bath or shower?', but it will indicate which official source would give the answer.

672 **European Access.**
Edited by Ian Thomson. London: Chadwyck Healey, 1989–
bi-monthly.

European Access is undoubtedly the foremost source of bibliography and current awareness in the UK. Although each issue includes well-written and authoritative articles by academics, professionals and EC officials, *Access* is based around a well-thought-out and easy-to-use index of official and commercial books, documents and journal articles in the two-month period covered by a given issue. Particularly valuable to researchers are the 'bibliographic reviews' which appear in each issue. Not only do these provide up-to-date references on their topic, but they will also give a concise and clear introduction to their chosen subject for the non-specialist.

673 **Basic sources of European Communities information.**
Barbara Zolynski, with contributions from Terry Hanson.
Nottingham, England: European Information Association, 1991. 35p.

Compiled by two highly experienced information professionals (Barbara Zolynski is EC librarian for the Law Society and Terry Hanson is Databases Officer for the European Information Association), this is an intensely practical guide to tracing information on the EC from both official and commercial sources.

674 **CCH Common Market Reporter.**
Bicester, England: CCH Editions, 1965– . fortnightly.

The structure of the *Reporter* is based on the Treaty of Rome and accompanying relevant treaties and conventions (such as treaties of accession, the Single European Act, judgment conventions). The provisions of the treaties and conventions are set out in full text and are accompanied by commentary and annotations, and, in the case of the Treaty of Rome, by relevant regulations and directives each with their own commentary. It includes a full case-reporting service and a regular survey of current EC developments. The work is indexed and is written by CCH editorial staff with occasional recourse to outside contributors. By November 1990 this loose-leaf publication had reached page 5500.

675 **CELEX.**
Eurobases. Brussels: Commission of the European Communities,
1951– .

Although not strictly a bibliography, CELEX (*Communitatis Europeae Lex*) is an invaluable and potent research tool. It is a computerized documentation system for Community law, the EC's legal database, and it covers all EC legislation from treaties to questions in the European Parliament. There are plans to extend the database to cover national transposition of directives and learned articles in the legal press. Searching CELEX in its full form is complex, and the services of a trained intermediary may be desirable – all EDCs and EICs may access CELEX. In the UK, CELEX is also available on the JUSTIS host and on CD-ROM.

676 **CORDIS (Community Research and Development Information Service).**
ECHO/Commission EC DGXIII, 1990– .

A new service incorporating a number of older databases, CORDIS provides easily searched on-line access to a full range of information on EC research and development (R&D) projects. Once complete, the service will offer: details of general R&D programmes; information on specific projects; abstracts from published results; details of R&D-related Commission working documents; news on research and contacts for further information and potential partners. Updates are regularly input from the ECHO host.

677 **ECLAS.**
Eurobases.   Brussels: Commission of the European Communities, 1990– .

ECLAS (European Commission's Library Automated System) is, in effect, the catalogue to the European Commission's central library available as an on-line database. Its content is very wide, including official publications, commercial books and journals, and academic theses.

678 **Eurocron.**
Eurobases/Statistical Office EC, 1991– .

A menu-driven service, providing access to Eurostat macroeconomic, regional and farm-structure data. Seven hundred tables of data are available, and the service updates regularly, depending on the file.

679 **RAPID.**
Eurobases.   Brussels: Commission of the European Communities, 1985– .

News publications have been filed daily in the RAPID database from 1985, and from 1990 this database has been available to the public. Within two hours of the daily midday Brussels briefing RAPID users will be able to read four types of documentary information on-line: P NOTES – press releases designed to present a basic summary and explanation of an important Commission policy proposal or decision; IP NOTES – these are usually shorter press releases announcing as a specific news item a Commission decision or statement intended to be of immediate impact or interest; MEMOS – background information notes addressed to journalists on a non-attributable basis; and selected speeches by members of the Commission, when these are available in fileable form.

680 **SCAD.**
Eurobases.   Brussels: Commission of the European Communities, 1983– .

SCAD (Système Communautaire d'Accès à la Documentation) is the bibliographical on-line database of the European Commission, and undoubtedly one of the most potent tools in this field. Anyone contemplating serious research should consider arranging for a SCAD search as a preliminary. The database covers EC documents (the principal legislation, together with all preparatory work), all secondary EC publications, articles from around 1,000 journals from all member states, and finally, statements on EC policy from both sides of industry. It is up-dated weekly.

Unfortunately no full text is available, but each entry includes an abstract of the item covered. All European Documentation Centres (EDCs) and Euro Info Centres (EICs) have access to this database, but it is usually advisable for researchers to make contact with their local centre to determine availability and search fees. *SCAD Bulletin* is the hardcopy version of the database, but it is very unwieldy.

681 **The Single Market: a guide to further reading.**
London: Department of Trade and Industry, 1991. 35p.

This guide lists publications on Single Market issues known to the British Department of Trade and Industry. It does not claim to be comprehensive, but it is certainly useful.

682 **Textline.**
London: Reuters, 1980– .

This constantly up-dated database offers full text, or substantial abstracts of stories from the leading newspapers in most EC member countries and beyond, together with Reuters' own wire services and the Agence Europe daily news service. Coverage is primarily concerned with economic, political and company-related news. Searching is highly flexible, including freetext and controlled language through an extensive system of codes.

Index

The index is a single alphabetical sequence of authors (personal and corporate), titles of publications and subjects. Index entries refer both to the main items and to other works mentioned in the note to each item. Title entries are in italics. Numbers refer to bibliographical entries.

161

171

179

181

182

Map of Western Europe

This map indicates the member states of the European Communities.

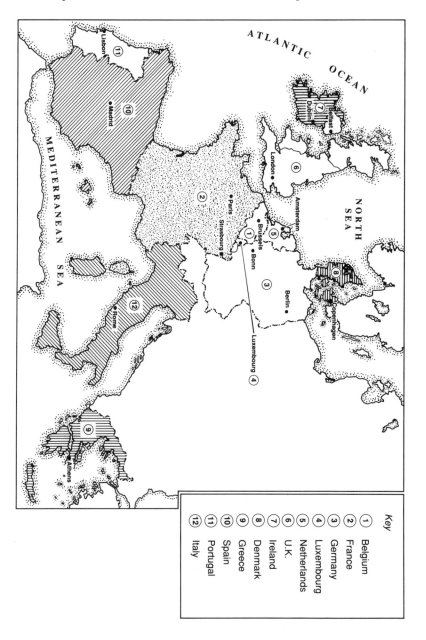

Key

1. Belgium
2. France
3. Germany
4. Luxembourg
5. Netherlands
6. U.K.
7. Ireland
8. Denmark
9. Greece
10. Spain
11. Portugal
12. Italy